'Fraser's approach to starting a business can help anyone get their ideas off the ground.'

JERRY GREENFIELD, co-founder of Ben & Jerry's

'This book will help you to stop thinking about starting a business and actually do it.'

JAMES WATT, Captain, BrewDog plc and
author of *Business for Punks*

'Launching a new business is one of the most intense and exhilarating things you can do. It doesn't have to take years of planning; Fraser's approach shows you how to get started today.'

MICHAEL ACTON SMITH, co-founder of
Mind Candy, Firebox and Calm

'Creating a great brand isn't easy, but Fraser shows that by having a clear and simple idea of what you want to say, there's no reason why time or money should hold you back.'

DAN GERMAIN, Group Head of Brand, Innocent

'The story of Fraser's success shows the importance of not getting tied up with over-thinking your ideas and proves you don't always need to re-invent the wheel.'

SIR TOM FARMER CVO, CBE, KCSG, DL, founder of Kwik-Fit

'48 hours, 2880 minutes, 172,800 seconds. Time's ticking. Don't waste it – there's no time like now!'

WILL KING, founder of King of Shaves

48-HOUR START-UP

48-HOUR START-UP

FROM IDEA TO LAUNCH IN 1 WEEKEND

FRASER DOHERTY

Thorsons

Thorsons
An imprint of HarperCollins*Publishers*
1 London Bridge Street
London SE1 9GF

www.harpercollins.co.uk

First published by Thorsons 2016

1 3 5 7 9 10 8 6 4 2

A catalogue record of this book is
available from the British Library

ISBN 978-0-00-819668-4

Printed and bound in Great Britain by
Clays Ltd, St Ives plc

MIX
Paper from
responsible sources
FSC™
www.fsc.org
FSC˚ C007454

DEDICATION

There are only two people that I need truly to thank for making my career as an entrepreneur a possibility. As a boy, I pitched thousands of business ideas to them. As a teenager, they patiently listened as I explained yet another hare-brained concept after another.

They never said 'no' and they never discouraged me. Never pressured me to walk a more familiar path and always let me seek out what I thought I was born to do.

All along the way, they did everything they could to make my dreams a reality. Waking up at 4am to drive me to the fruit market on a Monday. Or the farmers' market at the weekends. Or to a supermarket pitch far out of town. They stuck labels onto jars, served customers behind the stall and mucked in at the office.

They were there to lift my spirits when almost every one of my ideas failed, and to celebrate when a few of them worked. They were even willing to make an appearance on Korean TV, all to support their exhausting son.

I couldn't have done any of it without you, Mum and Dad.

CONTENTS

AUTHOR'S NOTE

Depending on the type of business you are hoping to start, doing so on a weekend may or may not be practical; for example, if you rely on getting materials from suppliers they may only be open on weekdays. To keep it simple, I have written *48-Hour Start-Up* over the course of Day 1 and Day 2. It's up to you whether you do yours during the week or at the weekend.

THE 48-HOUR START-UP PHILOSOPHY

For anyone with a dream to start up on their own, there are endless airport bookshops filled with 'build a billion-dollar company' manuals. But what if your dream isn't to build the next Apple? What if your dream is more … *realistic*?

For many of us, the most important thing that we are searching for in life is freedom. Freedom from the monotony of jobs we hate. Freedom to make a living doing something we love, to work the hours we want to work and to do business in whatever way feels right to us.

For me, starting a business to get rich somewhat misses the point. The adventure that I have had in growing my business – the fun I have had, people I've met and places I've visited – are the things that I treasure more than the material possessions I've been able to buy.

The idea that starting a business can be your route to freedom and adventure – to doing what you were born to do – can, for some people, be a slightly overwhelming prospect. A lot of people labour over their ideas, scheming and planning for years on end – with a worry that their idea isn't quite right yet, that maybe they need to do more market research to be completely sure that it won't be a total flop.

More than anything, this fear of failure stops people from pursuing their dreams. We hold ourselves back from what we deserve in life because we worry that if things don't work out as they should and we end up with egg on our faces, people will laugh – or worse, that they won't give us another chance.

Having met hundreds of people who struggle with this very real fear, it got me thinking: what if the risk of taking that plunge could be taken out of the equation? Is there, maybe, a way of starting a business that can allow people to dip their toe into the water, rather than jumping in at the deep end and risking everything? Perhaps if this were possible, I figured, more people would be willing and able to follow their hearts.

Maybe it's your dream to start a business and for it to become your new full-time career. Maybe you just want to try something out for a bit of fun on the side. Or perhaps you already have a business but want to find a way of testing out some new product ideas without betting the farm.

Whatever reason you have for taking on this experiment, I very much hope that the experiences, tools and tricks I have included in this book help you to get closer to your goals. I'm pretty confident that if you put in the focus and energy required, they will.

There are lessons I have learned and tools I have found that can make the process of going from idea to first customer a whole lot quicker. Although the businesses I have started – and indeed the business you will start – are all very different, many of the steps we all go through are almost exactly the same.

Because starting a business is a road that's been walked before, you'd be crazy to try to figure out every step of the route from scratch and on your own. Feel free to look at this book as a 'cheat sheet'; the basic essentials you need to know about the key steps of developing an idea and getting it to market quickly.

By hotwiring the whole start-up process in this way, you'll be able to do in days what most start-up entrepreneurs spend months on. Sure, you won't build a billion-dollar company in a weekend, but you'll be amazed at what you can achieve with a methodical process and, above all, two days of complete focus.

The progress you make in your first two days will most likely give you the confidence to take your idea even further. And, of course, the story of every successful company in the world began this way – someone overcame their fears and took the first step.

CHAPTER 1

ONE WEEKEND

'Is it possible to come up with an idea for a business and be up and running, selling a product to paying customers, all in the space of two days?'

This was the question that first started my journey with the 48-hour start-up, a slightly crazy experiment that I took on in the spring of 2016, without any real idea of what the outcome would be. I wanted to give it a shot, to see if the above challenge were possible to achieve, with all of the modern tools available to us entrepreneurs and by applying the many lessons I've learned so far in my exciting, challenging and at times down-right bizarre career in business.

Throughout my adventures as a young entrepreneur, I've had the pleasure of speaking at literally hundreds of entrepreneur events around the world. No matter how different the culture of the host country might be from my own, I have always felt at home in the company of other entrepreneurs. We are a sort of dysfunctional global family of people who just happen to think the same sort of way – people who don't want to work for someone else, but who want to make a mark on the world in our own particular way.

We're a group of people who like coming up with ideas, sometimes inventing products that hitherto didn't exist in the world. In my experience at least, we're also a group of people who tend to feel that life is short – that we ought to make the most of every second we have. For all kinds of reasons, we see starting a business as the best way of doing that – an opportunity to make a career for ourselves, maybe work with our friends, do something we love and perhaps in some small way change the world. What more could you want from your work?

But something I have found on my travels in this community is that not all of the people who feel this way actually do act on their emotions. In fact, most of the people who harbour such feelings live their lives in a fashion that contradicts them – they hold down a job, study at university, work towards a rise, pay their mortgages and generally go along with the status quo.

THE CULT OF WANTREPRENEURSHIP

Everywhere I've gone on my trips, speaking at different entre-preneurship events, I've been aware of the legions of 'wantrepre-neurs' who frequent such conferences. People who think a lot about starting a business – they attend the seminars, buy all the books, even meet with successful entrepreneurs to ask for advice … but they never actually start.

Perhaps they don't start out of fear of failure or maybe they just procrastinate, putting things off for another day. I am sure a lot of them are waiting for the 'perfect idea', which will never really come. They're always telling their friends about the idea-of-the-week, never giving enough focus to one idea for it to become anything close to a reality.

Far too often, wantrepreneurs will inhibit this very healthy process by keeping their ideas all bottled up to themselves, never even so much as sharing them with anyone – let alone actually getting them onto the market. I think this is all such a tragedy – no doubt all kinds of ideas don't make it into the world and, more importantly, so many people don't get the chance of taking them there.

Maybe some of these justifications for inaction sound familiar … and I don't want to be the one who says it but maybe, just maybe, the phrase 'wantrepreneur' applies to you. But don't worry, it's a very curable disease. I can assure you that if you're willing to take action then it's not a phrase that will describe you for much longer.

TELL EVERYONE YOUR IDEAS

There's something that, for me, absolutely sums up the wantrepreneur mentality. Quite often, at the end of one of my talks, people will come up to me and introduce themselves. They'll say, 'Hey, I have an idea for a business,' and I'll say, 'Oh, great, what's your idea?' … 'Oh no, I can't tell you that … what if you steal it?' they'll shriek.

Not only is this kinda funny, I think it is totally upside down. In my mind, if you have an idea for a business, especially if it's a half-baked one, you should tell anyone who'll listen – you never know which person might help you. They might give you some useful feedback or introduce you to someone who works in your industry or if you're very lucky, point you in the direction of a willing customer.

Because people keep their cards close to their chests in this slightly misguided way, I never do get to hear all of these ideas. I should probably be careful what I say because, for all I know, some of these people I've met are working on truly revolutionary, paradigm-shifting, world-changing innovations. The chances are, however, that they're not.

And that's not just me being mean. I'm sure you're well aware that the likelihood of any idea going anywhere is pretty slim – most new businesses barely make it off the starting blocks and, more often than not, the ones that do are destined to fail.

So, in light of the terrible odds facing these bright-eyed entrepreneurs, the chances of their businesses making it are, at least in my opinion, even more slim. If their ideas haven't so much as had the oxygen of discussion, they really don't stand a fighting chance.

PESSIMISM AND OPTIMISM

Ideas are extremely precious little things. You can absolutely assume that the first incarnation of any idea is completely wrong – that it needs more bashing about, further iterations, until it actually makes sense. I sometimes think that the perfect environment for an idea to succeed is one with equal parts of blind optimism and honest pessimism.

Let me explain what I mean by this. First off, there's definitely a need for a little bit of blind faith in the recipe of what makes an idea succeed. If you analyse any idea enough, you'll soon put yourself off starting it at all. The thing is that most ideas don't make a lot of sense in the beginning. It's only by having the faith of actually getting them going and learning as you go that you'll wind up hitting upon a model that works.

Because of this, you need to have a bit of faith – throw yourself completely into your idea even if it isn't all perfectly mapped out at the start. So many wantrepreneurs are waiting to complete a business plan or do more market research – the truth is that your idea will never be perfectly formed before it gets out into the world. Basically, you just need to start.

Coupled with this faith, you need your idea to go through a bit of a beating. If nothing else, you need to talk to a few people to be sure that you're not completely crazy … or at least that your idea isn't. You will be tempted to simply ask your family and friends what they think, but the fact is that they aren't really going to give you impartial advice – they love you too much to tell you honestly if your idea stinks.

So, you need to try running your idea past some people who have been there and done it before or some people who are inside your chosen industry who know what they're talking about. You need to find some people who aren't afraid of hurting your feelings, people who don't have any kind of vested interest in you or your idea.

This process doesn't need to take a lot of time and, of course, later in the book we will talk about some of the ways that you can find this critique very quickly. If you can muster up enough optimism to throw yourself wholeheartedly into your idea and also find some pessimists to help bash it into shape, your little caterpillar of a concept might well grow into a beautiful butterfly.

Of course, some of your ideas will be beaten to death by pessimism – and perhaps quite rightly. Never be too pig-headed to change your idea or change your mind. If all the advice comes back as a thumbs-down, maybe consider your other options.

No matter how many ideas you have to go through, the most important thing is that you maintain your optimism. I guarantee that if you do that, eventually you'll make a start and you'll graduate from wantrepreneur to entrepreneur.

MY START AS AN ENTREPRENEUR

In my case, I always wanted to be an entrepreneur, perhaps from an unusually young age. I'm not exactly sure where it started but I was always making things and selling thing to the neighbours.

My earliest memory of trying to make money was from when I was about eight years old. I baked some cakes and sold them to my teachers at school. I sent the money that I made to Greenpeace, my favourite charity at the time. By ten, my entrepreneurial ambitions had grown and I was fascinated by the simple businesses that I came across as a child on the outskirts of my home town of Edinburgh. I visited a local chicken farm with a childhood friend. 'What a great business!' I thought: the farmer just has to feed the chickens, they lay eggs, and he can carefully steal them to sell for a profit, without having to share any of the takings with his feathered employees. Bingo!

We convinced the farmer to give us a box of eggs for free, which I took home to my mum and dad and explained that we'd had this brilliant business idea. We would keep the eggs warm so that they would hatch and then sell the eggs that the resulting brood of chickens would lay!

As I'm sure you can imagine, my parents weren't particularly keen on this business idea – of turning their suburban back garden into a chicken farm! Fairly used to my hare-brained schemes by this point, however, they let us give it a shot, not really expecting two ten-year-old boys could find a way of hatching eggs.

And so we put the eggs on top of the cable TV box under the telly, where it was kind of warm. And, amazingly, three weeks later, four of the eggs hatched into little chickens. The poor things probably thought that Jerry Springer was their mum!

We raised the chickens in the house, gave them names, and soon they were big enough to go out into a house my dad built for them in the garden. Before long, they were laying eggs, which we sold to the neighbours.

Unfortunately, my chicken farming career was sadly cut short one afternoon when the local fox decided to eat the chickens for dinner! I guess you could say that I learned my first real lesson as an entrepreneur – that, at the absolute least, you should look for a business idea that doesn't have any natural predators!

As I'm sure you can tell by this point, my beloved parents were very supportive of my no doubt exhausting entrepreneurial energy as a child. My interests baffled them, and everyone around us. Neither of my parents nor anyone we knew had ever started a business before – where this interest came from was something of a mystery.

FROM EGGS TO BACON

It wasn't long before I met an entrepreneur for the first time. One of my high school friends had a job as a 'bacon boy', selling bacon and sausages door to door. He told me about how he was paid 30p commission for each packet of bacon that he sold. I was instantly hooked – where could I sign up?

My friend explained that since I was only 12 this would be a problem – I would have to pretend that I was 13. 'No problem,' I exclaimed. And so it was arranged that my friend would introduce me to the boss – The Bacon Man, a Mr Alan Bryson. Despite my naïvety and perhaps the insincerity of some of my answers, I got the job, and within days we were pounding the concrete, knocking on doors all over the neighbourhood.

It didn't take long for me to build up a list of regular customers. I would walk miles every evening after school, proudly wearing my white uniform and always trying to improve my pitch. In the beginning I was selling maybe 20 packets a week, but gradually I found myself close to breaking the 50-packet-a-week mark.

TEENAGED COMPETITION

The Bacon Man published a weekly newsletter for his fifty or so teenaged, spotty sales reps. He would include motivational quotes – 'If you fail to plan, you should plan to fail,' that sort of thing – along with a 'Top 10' table of who had grossed the most sales that week.

A few months into the job, I found myself published in the top ten for the first time. My sense of achievement was immense – I had grown my delivery route to include all of the well-to-do neighbourhoods in the west of Edinburgh. It wasn't an easy job and I worked hard at it. I would walk down vast driveways in the rain, only to be told that the owners were Muslim, Jewish, on holiday, on a diet or just didn't have any money to hand.

Eventually, at around 60 packets sold in one week, I found myself in second place with another boy. His name was Richard Field; I can remember his name to this day. He had beaten me by only a few packs – next week I was resolved to top the charts.

But I quickly learned that he wasn't going to give up the top spot easily, and so found myself engaged in a spate of competitive bacon selling.

Our weekly totals rapidly touched 80 packets apiece and continued to climb. One week he would have the top spot; the next it would be mine. Eventually, partly thanks to the modest innovation of doing my round by bicycle instead of on foot, I managed to overtake him for good. This competition resulted in an achievement I still feel a twinge of pride over: I became the first Bacon Boy to sell 100 packets in a week!

Impressed by my accomplishment, the Bacon Man asked me to become his new right-hand man. I was 13 years old and nobody so young had been granted such an honour before. The deal was that he'd pick me up from school in his van and drop me off in an area of town I'd never been to. I'd be given an under-performing Bacon Boy and it would be my task to get them up to speed.

What a wonderful job, I thought. And that wasn't all: I'd be paid the incredible sum of £20 a day. An unheard-of amount among the kids of our playground.

'Sounds great!' I thought. 'No way!' my parents shrieked. Whether they didn't like the idea of me wandering through the wrong parts of town in the dark, or were concerned that all this extracurricular bacon selling would affect my studies, I'm not sure, but my parents' reservations stood no chance against my enthusiasm, and I was soon selling bacon wherever it needed to be sold. The Bacon Man taught me everything he knew. He was truly an archetypal entrepreneur – a man who saw an opportunity and went for it, regardless of how unconventional a business model it no doubt appeared to his friends when he first started 'The Bacon Service'.

He taught me the basics of customer service. He would go crazy if he found out that a Bacon Boy hadn't been doing his 'call backs'. This was where you would have to walk back to a house of one of your regular customers at the end of your round – if they had been out the first time you called. Of course, this was a total pain in the ass, especially if they were still out the second time around.

But the lesson he taught me was that if you didn't get hold of your customer, you had let them down. Some, for example, were old ladies who counted on your delivery each week. They would often have the correct change all ready for you. If they had popped out to the post-box and ended up missing their bacon that week, there was a risk they'd buy a multipack at the supermarket instead and you would lose them forever.

KEEP ON KNOCKING

The bacon-selling job was a truly formative experience, and the attitude it pressed into me has had an impact on me to this day.

There is no more physically exhausting and mentally gruelling way to sell a product than by going door to door with it piled high in a plastic bucket. At least if you do telesales you have a seat.

Add to that the fact that there can't be many more unpleasant climates in which to go door-to-door selling than the one we have here in Scotland. For the most part, it was so cold outside that the bacon we were selling needed no further refrigeration!

Our customers were Scottish housewives – a thrifty bunch who knew the prices of equivalent products in the supermarket only too well. It's safe to say that a Bacon Boy faces more than his fair share of rejection on his rounds.

We would knock on nine doors before the tenth might say 'yes', taking a packet from our shivering hands and replacing it with a few coins. At first, being rejected over and over again was hard to take. But in the end I came to accept that as a Bacon Boy, just as in life, you have to knock on thousands of doors, each time with the same enthusiasm as the last. For the most part, anyone's career as an entrepreneur is a sea of rejection, peppered with the occasional hard-won sale. A process of trying something, failing, changing tack a little and trying again. This is natural.

My youthful sales experience provided me with a great education. I was totally captivated by the whole world of starting a business – amazed that through nothing more than walking the streets, pressing doorbells and talking to people, I could build a business out of thin air, despite my being a teenager who knew nothing about anything. I could secure hundreds of regular customers and even grow my little enterprise week on week, simply by doing a good job.

Remember, at the start of your 48-hour journey, the importance of starting small. There is no shame in launching a product on a tiny scale – at a farmers' market, or by picking up the phone, or, heaven forbid, knocking on doors.

In the end, despite my fondness for the Bacon Man and the lessons he was teaching me, I had a burning desire to 'stick it to the Man'. Why was I spending my life working for someone else when I now knew how to do it on my own?

The urge towards self-employment overtook me and I soon resigned from the Bacon Service, telling the boss I would be striking out on my own. Entrepreneurship had come knocking.

BE WILLING TO TRY

All of these early experiences as a kid really shaped my attitude in business to this day. I was very lucky to have parents who stressed to my brother Connor and me that the most important thing in life was to find something that we loved – that to get up in the morning and do something you enjoy is success. They never tried to push us into a particular direction and always supported us, no matter how bizarre our dreams at the time might have been.

Looking back, I'm amazed that my parents showed such patience throughout my eccentric childhood attempts at making money. I've come to learn as an adult that most parents wouldn't have put up with such things. They tend not to let their kids raise farmyard animals in the family home. Fair enough, I suppose. More seriously, they typically tell kids that their ideas won't work. They short-circuit the process – rather than letting their kids learn from trying and failing, they'd rather they didn't try at all.

Through the Bacon Man I gained a basic understanding of what it meant to be an entrepreneur. He was someone who approached life on his own terms, and actually enjoyed what he did, almost obsessively so.

Thanks to his bacon empire, he was able to go on three or four holidays a year and, at least by my calculations as a naïve teenager, he barely had to do any work – the grunt work (excuse the pun) was done by his loyal teenaged followers.

Thanks to my slightly unconventional childhood, my life has been one of hundreds of small business failures and a few successes. I've attempted all kinds of ideas over the years, and most of them didn't work.

Throughout my teens, I tried more than I care to remember. Most I have tried to banish from my mind, having wasted months on them barking up the wrong tree. Some memorable experiences include an attempt to redesign nappies so that they could be flushed down the toilet rather than sent to landfill, a business selling bars of chocolate with teachers' faces printed on them, and a company distributing biodegradable plastic cups to outdoor events. I made websites for people, printed funny T-shirts and even brewed my own beer. In my twenties I tried various other ventures – delivering healthy meals for the elderly; creating a last-minute high-end restaurant booking app; launching a healthy food subscription business – and invested my savings in all kinds of other people's start-up ideas, most of which didn't make a return.

When I ask people what they think of all of this, they usually reflect on how I have been able to bounce from one failure to the next, without losing enthusiasm for the overall project of being an entrepreneur. My parents always seemed delighted, if not a little puzzled, that, even when I was a child, within days of giving up one unsuccessful concept I would already be working on some other idea that I was convinced would change the world. This, I believe, is because I am not afraid of giving ideas a shot, even if there is a high possibility of failure. I absolutely have my parents to thank for that – for never discouraging me from trying.

MY FIRST WEEKEND AS AN ENTREPRENEUR

You may already know a little about my SuperJam story from my earlier book, *SuperBusiness*, in which I shared the adventure that I went on 'from my gran's kitchen to the supermarket shelves and beyond'.

After my short career with The Bacon Service, I found myself looking everywhere for a new business idea and then, one afternoon, my grandmother was making jam in her kitchen in Glasgow, just as she had for as long as I can remember. Eureka! Jam would be my product.

We made a few jars together, Gran sharing her jam-making secrets with me, and then, bursting with enthusiasm, I raced to the supermarket to buy some fruit to make a few jars of my own. While the fruit was boiling I printed some labels on the computer at home, under the imaginative-enough brand name 'Doherty's Preserves'. I adorned the jars with a little strip of tartan ribbon, stolen from my mum's sewing box.

Before the bubbling jam with which I had filled the odd-shaped jars had even cooled down, I headed out to the streets with a dozen or so loaded into a plastic bucket. I strained under the weight of them as I walked from house to house. Almost everyone said no, but eventually a kind old lady who knew me from my days of selling bacon bought a jar. I was in business!

I could barely contain my excitement as she counted out her £1.80 in small coins into my hand. I no doubt beamed with enthusiasm as I knocked on door after door after door that cold Scottish evening. An hour or two later I returned to my parents, proudly holding the plastic bucket upside down over my head – I was triumphant! Before long, my success was such that the *Edinburgh Evening News* ran a story about me at 15 years old.

From that point on, jam completely took over my life, to the point that I decided to leave school and go full time into making it. I'm not sure whether my parents thought it would truly become my career, but they could see I was doing something I loved, and that was what mattered.

I was soon making jam every day, selling it at farmers' markets all over Scotland. I constantly tweaked my recipes, learning from customers as they gave me feedback on the previous weeks' batch. A lot of people told me that they didn't eat jam because it has so much sugar in it. This simple market feedback gave me an idea. What if I could create a recipe for jam that was made 100 per cent from fruit? And so I experimented in the kitchen for months and months, trying everything I could think of –

making jam completely from fruit, with honey instead of sugar, until eventually I settled on a combination of fruit and fruit juice.

It became my dream to sell my latest idea – which I quickly named SuperJam – to the major supermarkets. I convinced my dad to drive me to the head office of Waitrose, having heard that they host special events called 'Meet the Buyer Days', where hundreds of people show up, brandishing their homemade cakes and soups and sauces. Everyone gets ten minutes to pitch their idea, in my case to the 'Senior Jam Buyer' – I bet you had no idea that such a job title existed!

While my dad waited in the car outside, I told the buyer all about my idea for making jam 100 per cent from fruit. He said it was an excellent idea and a lot of fun to see a 16-year-old boy presenting it. (I'd borrowed my dad's suit for the occasion, probably two sizes too big for me, which no doubt provided the buyer with some amusement!)

Although he liked my jam, he told me very straightforwardly that the business idea is only a small part of the equation of what makes a product a success. He explained that I would have to set up production in a factory and offer him a good price. I'd have to get labels designed that explained to people why they should buy my products. And I'd have to do a bit more work on my recipes before he'd be happy.

This was my biggest rejection to date. I should have learned by then that the first time I knocked on the door of a big supermarket, they probably wouldn't say yes. I was totally bummed out for I had absolutely no idea how to create a brand and set up production in a factory.

LESSONS LEARNED

While I had managed to start the first incarnation of my jam business quite literally in a weekend, with little more than a wooden spoon and a big helping of teenaged optimism, the next step wasn't going to happen so fast. The task of creating a 'real business', a product that genuinely had the potential to make it big, seemed insurmountable. And such fears seemed confirmed when I returned to the buyer a year later to meet with another rejection. The buyer explained that the labels I had created were too silly, the factory too expensive and my recipes too unusual. Basically, I'd got everything wrong and had to start all over again!

Although I was totally devastated, I had come to accept that rejection would always be a big part of this process. I also learned that while family and friends are an extremely important source of help and support, they're not able to give impartial advice. When they see you fail, they hate to see you get hurt and so would rather that you stopped. The person you should actually listen to, and I know it sounds cheesy, is the customer. In my case, even though I had done everything wrong, the buyer still felt that I had a good idea.

If everyone tells you that your idea stinks, including customers, you should probably reassess whether or not it is the right thing to be doing with your life. But if customers still maintain that your idea is something they'd be interested in buying, there's a good chance that you should keep going. That glimmer of hope helped me to persevere.

And thank God, because it did turn out to be a good idea. By the time I redesigned the labels and convinced a new factory to work with me, the supermarket said 'Yes', and before long we had launched in more than 1,000 stores around the world and SuperJam was entered into the National Museum of Scotland as an example of an 'Iconic Scottish Brand'.

A personal highlight of my adventure was seeing SuperJam become something of a phenomenon in South Korea. For my grandmother the biggest day out was our visit to Buckingham Palace, where we were presented with a medal by Prince Charles. But what I enjoyed most was seeing my life story made into a TV drama in Japan. In the dramatised re-enactment, I was played by a small Indian boy – something, presumably, was lost in translation, but never mind!

SuperJam has been something of an adventure and a success, but I can't help wondering sometimes how much more quickly it could all have been achieved. During the process, I found that every facet of setting up a real business was new to me. I had no idea how to create a brand, how to work out the finances or anything else. I really knew nothing, and had to figure it all out as I went along, taking many a wrong turn and wasting priceless months as I did.

Of course, when I came to apply lessons learned to my second business and then to my third, the whole process became a lot quicker – I simply didn't make the same mistakes again.

ENVELOPE COFFEE

One of my best friends is Lennart Clerkx; he's Dutch, and a pretty interesting guy – able to speak seven languages. But one of the things that is a little unusual about him is that he doesn't have any sense of smell. That's a serious affliction. However, it's not all bad news. Just as those who are blind sometimes have extra good hearing to sort of compensate, so Lennie has unusually good taste buds. He can pick up on the acidity or sweetness of what he's eating better than most people.

He discovered that he had this particular talent, and subsequently became interested in coffee, when he was living in Denmark, where some of the world's most pioneering roasters are based. Now, he's made a whole career out of his taste buds.

Coffee roasters from around Europe send him to Africa, and Central and South America, in search of the best beans. He can tell better than anyone how acidic or sweet a particular harvest is. He's also all about paying the growers a fair price for these incredible beans that he discovers. His company, This Side Up, helps small roasters buy beans from these far-flung places, directly from the farmers.

Not long after we first met, sharing a beer by a canal, Lennie told me all about his travels in the developing world and I became instantly fascinated. He showed me photos of the places he'd visited and told me about the lives of the farmers. More than anything, he was evangelical about how great their coffees were.

On another weekend visit to see him in Amsterdam, and no doubt after a few more beers, we decided there was a better way to do the coffee business. Why didn't we buy the beans directly from the farmers, using Lennie's connections, and then sell the roasted coffee directly to customers over the internet? No middlemen, no importers and no supermarkets between our customers and the people growing these incredible beans.

Within a matter of days I had come up with the name 'Envelope Coffee'. I'd found a local coffee roaster in Glasgow who could roast and pack the beans for us and had set up a simple website to charge our customers a fortnightly subscription.

Using a list of ethically sourced beans from countries such as Rwanda and Ecuador, we soon had a product to sell. We used standard coffee envelopes, which we ordered inexpensively online, but made them look great by creating a nice label for them.

I invited a Danish photographer, Kiva Brynaa, to London to shoot the product *in situ* at a coffee roaster's premises over the course of a half-day. Even though the company had been started on a shoestring in a matter of days, I wanted our customers to get the best possible impression of us. In my opinion, brilliant photography can ensure this in a way that nothing else can. I really believe that foods – especially things like coffee – are visual products. We eat with our eyes.

Within weeks of having the idea for Envelope Coffee, we sold our first bag of coffee. And it didn't take long before we had a loyal base of subscribers – the product truly spoke for itself. Besides, coffee is a pretty addictive product – when you find one you like, you stick with it.

Buoyed by one another's enthusiasm for the project, within weeks Lennie and I were on a flight to Colombia to find our beans. We took another Danish friend, Nick Levin, a photographer and filmmaker, to shoot a short movie about Colombian coffee.

Over there, they grow some of the best coffee in the world and they're very proud of it. After a night in the big city of Bogotá, we headed to the countryside. When we got there, we spent some time with Juan Pablo, one of Colombia's foremost coffee experts – a man who tastes more than 600 cups of coffee … a day!

While we were waiting for a sample batch of beans to roast in a tiny roaster, I asked him what he drank on his breaks, which I meant as a joke. 'Oh, coffee,' he said, with an air of bemusement. He drank up to 16 cups of coffee when he wasn't at work. He later told us that he got all of two hours' sleep a night – and that the rest of the time he was thinking about coffee.

This guy was full of energy. And in his office, with him, we tasted more than 100 of the best coffees from around Colombia. We found one that we particularly loved – it was perfect for what we were looking for. So we decided that we would shake hands with the farmer, cut out the middlemen and buy the coffee directly from him. A simple idea, or so we thought.

We soon found ourselves in an unfamiliar country about which we had heard all kinds of horror stories. Two flights into the Andes later and an eight-hour drive along a treacherous cliff-face of a road, we found ourselves in the most beautiful little village I've ever seen. It was situated 1,200 metres above sea level – very high up in the mountains. The village was at the foot of a volcano, so the soil was incredibly fertile, perfect for growing coffee. The fruit was falling out of the trees and there was coffee growing everywhere – Lennie was in coffee heaven!

There were over 1,000 people living in the village, all completely reliant on the coffee harvest for their livelihoods. And they were very happy to see us. Until relatively recently the area hadn't been safe enough for international coffee buyers like us to visit – mostly because of cocaine production, smuggling and guerrilla activity endemic to the area.

But now it was safe for people like us to explore the fields, and the farmers showed us their plots with pride. We found a particular farm that we really liked – the plants were very well taken care of, with plenty of shade, and the family who owned them were wonderful. We stayed in their home for a few days and enjoyed eating the local cuisine – although we did turn down their offer of barbecued guinea-pig.

In the end, we bought their beans and shipped them to Scotland for roasting. Not only did we have some of the world's best coffee on our hands, we also had this great story to tell about the people we'd bought it from and the beautiful place where they'd grown it.

I was so confident that people would like our coffee that we offered anyone their first bag 'on the house'. I placed vouchers in hundreds of thousands of magazines that I thought the right kind of people would buy. We rewarded customers who shared our offer with their friends.

Over the course of a few months, around 10,000 coffee-lovers signed up for our club. The reviews for our Colombian coffee were outstanding. Our business soon attracted the attention of a larger competitor, who offered to buy us out.

By this point, my own time was so stretched between SuperJam and other projects that this seemed like the best option. I wasn't putting the kind of time into Envelope that would be needed to take it from a lifestyle business into a 'real company'. I was, however, very proud of this fantastic product that we made.

I definitely now believe in the importance of focusing on one idea at a time. As entrepreneurs, it's easy to be like a magpie. Always distracted by the latest shiny idea.

What amazed me about this experience of starting Envelope was that I managed to go from having an idea with my friend in the pub to having a great product in people's hands in a remarkably short space of time. Not only had we done it fast, we'd also done it well. Anyone looking at our site wouldn't have thought the company has been started in only a few weeks – our photography was beautiful, our packaging was just as good as any of our competitors' and, most importantly, the product was delicious.

BEER52

A similar business that I was involved in starting is Beer52, a craft beer club. My now business partner James Brown had been on a motorcycle road trip around Europe with his dad, during which they'd stopped at craft beer bars and breweries, refreshing themselves along the way.

The way I tell that makes it sound like they were drink-driving but I promise you they weren't!

This trip ignited James's passion for craft beer and on his return to Scotland he started to learn more and more about the beers and breweries he had found on his trip. With the help of some quick internet research, he learned that there are more than 14,000 microbreweries in the world. They are literally popping up everywhere, with new ones opening every week. The craft beer trend is a well-documented success story all over the world.

But with so many breweries out there, how could anyone even begin to discover the best ones? Most of them are just selling in their local area on a small scale.

James decided that he wanted to do something about this – create a way for people to discover some of these great beers and also a way for the breweries to get their beers out to a wider audience.

We met up and threw some ideas around. Wouldn't it be cool to make a sort of tasting club, we figured. We could ring up breweries and ask for samples, then together we could have fun tasting the hundreds of bottles that came in and pick the best ones. Once we'd figured out which were the best, we'd order a whole batch to send out to our members. Sounds like a fun business!

And so the idea for Beer52 was born. We would produce a monthly selection of craft beers from around the world and deliver a mixed case of bottles directly to our customers' doors. They'd pay a monthly subscription to be in the club and we'd produce tasting notes and content about the beers, so that people could learn all about what they were drinking.

Selling beer on the internet

Neither of us really knew how to build a full-on subscription website from scratch, but the great thing was that we didn't have to. We used a service called Shopify to make a very simple website (there are lots of these services available, so check out which one is best for you).

We hired a freelance designer to create a simple logo, then mocked up an example of how we wanted our boxes to look and booked a photographer to create some images for the site. Within almost no time we had gone from having an idea to creating a website that gave the impression we were an established brand.

With the basic building blocks in place, we immediately started calling up breweries to ask if they'd sell us, say, 100 bottles of beer for us to send out in our deliveries to our customers. For the most part, they didn't return our calls. It wasn't a large enough size of order for them.

So we tried a different angle. We rang breweries and asked if they would send us 1,000 bottles of their beer for free. In return, we'd get it out into the hands of people who love craft beer. The breweries found these kinds of numbers much more exciting and agreed to give it a shot.

Samples started arriving within days and we had the oh-so-difficult task of deciding which were our favourites to put into our inaugural selection box. We arranged for the beer to be delivered to a third-party fulfilment centre – a place that had the ability to store and pack our orders as they came through, simply charging us a small fee for each one that went out the door.

In the end, we produced 1,500 cases for our launch. It was a bold move but we knew that for a subscription business we would need to attract a critical mass of members – only some of those who took up our initial offer would go on to become loyal members.

To attract this initial critical mass we knew we would have to do something more than just hand out some fliers in the street; it would take a bolder and more unconventional initiative to get 1,500 people to sign up for our club in the first month. We came up with the idea of using Groupon.

Normally, people would say that using a discount website to launch your business amounts to suicide. Surely that's the sort of place that great brands go to face their deaths, not their births.

But the way we saw it was that there was no better way to get our launch into the email inboxes of millions of people from day one. By giving them a special deal on their first box – just £9 instead of the usual £24, hopefully a large number of people would take it up. And, assuming our product was any good, hopefully enough would stay into the following month to pay full price.

The deal launched. Within 40 minutes we had sold out of beer. We were so excited and the people at Groupon were too – they'd never sold beer before on their site so perhaps we had helped them to discover a whole new category of opportunity. Now all we had to do was to send the orders across to the warehouse to be shipped to our customers.

If only it were that simple – we had never shipped glass bottles of beer before and hadn't thoroughly tested our packaging, in our rush to get our product to market. Within days we were flooded with hundreds of complaints – about a third of the packages had arrived smashed at our customers' doors. Not really an ideal way for our brand to introduce itself to the world.

In the end we replaced all of the broken bottles and refunded those customers. A lot of them were so impressed by how we handled the problem that they've stayed with us to this day. We went on to improve our packaging and have since seen more than 100,000 members join our club.

We've sold many millions of bottles of beer and worked with hundreds of the most pioneering breweries from around the world. Our magazine, *Ferment*, is the largest-circulation publication on craft beer in the country and we've been able to raise investment to launch our brand internationally.

I think what made this business work was that we just ran with an idea. We didn't sit around planning things out perfectly – we just picked up the phone to breweries and tried to sell them our concept. When they didn't like our initial idea, we changed it instantly.

Sure, when we launched it wasn't plain sailing but we did go from zero to over 1,000 customers in a day. As the business has developed, we've continued to apply these same principles. We're constantly testing ideas very fast and on very small budgets. If things work, we scale them up. If they don't, we scrap them and move on.

Human behaviour

Another one of the reasons for Beer52's success is that we used a business model that fitted well with our customers' natural habits. I know in my own life that if I sign up for a subscription, unless I don't like what I'm being sent, I am usually happy just to let it run and run.

If our customers had to come to our website every month to place an order, they'd probably buy less on average than if they have a subscription set up. Partly because they share my laziness but also because a subscription can be a really convenient way of receiving a regular supply of something you enjoy, especially if it's something as easily consumed as beer!

Beer52's customers have a high lifetime value, because when someone signs up they're not just buying one box of beer; they're typically subscribing for a large number of months. Thanks to this, we can spend a lot of money on marketing upfront to attract customers to sign up in the first place.

YOU AREN'T ALONE

What we've learned is that it's possible to have an idea in the pub one night and develop it into a business the next, with a credible website registered to a catchy domain name for all the world to see. This can all be done extremely quickly – and that means by the competition as much as by you.

A phenomenon that I've observed countless times is that whenever we've been working on a new idea – one that we thought was totally original – we weren't alone. Someone else in the world has read the same articles, maybe has the same interests and has started thinking about how to solve the same problems.

Often, products come to market at almost the same time, and one looks like a carbon copy of the other. Sometimes they are exactly that – a fast-follower – but quite often they're part of this phenomenon of simultaneous invention. With all of our ideas – our beer club, our coffee club and many of the new products that we have presented to retailers through SuperJam – the competition has created exactly the same concepts at or around the same time.

The idea of a craft beer club didn't exist a few years ago but at the last count there were more than ten in the UK alone, all started within a short space of each other. While we're by far the largest, there are certainly a lot of upstarts following fast on our heels.

It's my belief that, in this environment, our only defence is to move more quickly than the rest. Whatever your idea is, the chances are that someone else is already working on it. So if you can give yourself a head start by getting off the ground first, that could make all the difference between success and failure. There's nothing worse than planning your idea for months and months only to be pipped to the post by someone launching their version before you.

STARTING UP FAST

Especially during my time creating SuperJam, I had a lot of ups and downs, and there were plenty of times when I reached a dead end and thought of giving up. With Envelope and Beer52, there were also steep learning curves – all kinds of things that I didn't know about selling online and creating internet businesses.

But each time I have set up a business, the process has got faster and faster. I've learned that even if the products you are trying to sell are completely different, many of the processes you need to go through are exactly the same.

Having done things the 'hard way', I wondered whether it was possible to short-circuit the lengthy process of coming up with a successful product and bringing it to market. I wanted to see if I could get something off the ground and have money coming through the checkout at lightning speed, ideally in just two days, from a starting point of nothing.

Based on the mistakes I'd made while growing SuperJam and starting other businesses, I knew there must be an easier way of doing things. Over those ten years, I had figured out how to outsource manufacturing, get great design work produced, handle customer service and arrange photo-shoots, and had learned all kinds of other bits and pieces necessary for creating a business. All things that I didn't study beforehand but that I figured out through trial and error.

SHOESTRING BUDGETS

Starting a business can be an incredibly expensive process. That's if you do things the conventional way. By the time you pay for designers, lawyers, accountants, stock, printing, web development, domain names and office space, I'd be surprised if you had any change left out of ten grand.

And that's money down the drain before a penny has even gone through the checkout. If your business idea proves unsuccessful, you stand to lose a huge amount of money.

I wondered whether there might be a smarter way of doing these things – a way to avoid many of the normal costs involved in starting a business. If so, that would mean it was no longer such a big deal if it didn't work – you could just go back to the drawing board and try something else, armed with the lessons you've learned from your first idea failing.

Ideally, I wanted to take an idea to market for a few hundred pounds – not because I don't have more capital at my disposal, but because I wanted to show that it could be done. If you can start a business for such a small amount of money, surely that would mean that anybody could do it?

Very often, wantrepreneurs use a 'lack of capital' as a scapegoat for not starting their business right away. They create vast shopping lists of all the things they believe they need – an office, a world-class design agency to create their brand, an all-singing-all-dancing website. Surely you don't need all those things to at least get a product onto the market?

THE 48-HOUR START-UP

Despite wanting to 'bootstrap' my 48-hour start-up and build a website for very little money, it was important to me that it was still well designed and professional. Most of all, my product would have to be a good one that people would actually want to buy. There is definitely a bare minimum in terms of design and quality that your product needs to achieve.

Starting a new business has to be something that creatively is an exciting project to work on, otherwise what's the point? Besides, if you're not working on something you love, then when the going gets tough you'll quit at the first hurdle.

Given that I have previously launched products that hundreds of thousands of people have loved, this new start-up would have to be of the same calibre – I wanted it to make people go 'wow'. Otherwise, perhaps, it would be what musicians call 'the dreaded second album'; my peers would have an expectation of what sort of business I might start, and if it fell short of that it wouldn't look so good. I'm sure that you too want any business you build to be something you can be proud to show your friends.

Most of all, however, I needed to create a business model that would require a minimum amount of input from me in the months and years that followed its creation, because of my exist-ing business commitments.

I wanted to find a way for the business to be outsourced, streamlined and automated. After a customer placed an order, I wanted the whole process to be handled without any input on my part. The order would be placed online, sent to a third-party warehouse for packing, and then delivered to the customer by courier.

Rather than using expensive design agencies, I found inexpensive freelancers online who were willing to create my branding and advertising for a fraction of the cost. Using highly measurable forms of marketing, such as Google AdWords, I was able to promote my start-up on a tiny budget, knowing that for every pound I spent on marketing, a new customer would click 'buy'.

Using this 'virtual' business model, where the company has no premises or staff of its own and only uses forms of marketing that can be measured and automated, the business could be extremely scalable – it wouldn't be limited by the amount of time that I could invest in it.

Very often, people feel their idea has to be perfect right from the start. Actually, I am a huge believer in making a simple version of your concept that is 'good enough' and just getting going, making changes and improvements on the fly.

Rather than spending weeks trying to come up with the perfect name, you'll pick one that does the trick in a matter of minutes. Instead of creating a brand that is a work of art, spending tens of thousands of dollars along the way, you will be happy to pay someone a few hundred dollars to create something that helps you bring in your first few customers, maybe investing in improvements in the future when you can more easily afford to.

A NEW ERA

What's really cool is that we are at the advent of a new dawn of entrepreneurship. While it used to cost huge amounts of money and take months to start a new business, the internet and the new tools that it brings have increasingly made it possible for anyone to start a business in their bedroom that competes with the biggest companies of the day, for almost no money.

You need little more than an idea and a willingness to give it a shot. This is such a revolution that thousands of people are starting businesses from the comfort of their own homes every week. They're fortunate enough to be making a living out of doing what they love – something that just wasn't possible even a few years ago.

The cost of starting a business has been driven through the floor by online tools and marketplaces that help first-time entrepreneurs find freelancers, products and customers in a matter of clicks.

Services like Shopify allow you to get a professional website online in hours, for no upfront cost and just a low monthly fee. Upwork (formerly oDesk) and various skills marketplaces put you in touch with freelance designers, writers, marketers and developers, bypassing expensive agencies with their flashy city-centre offices. Moo allows you to design your own printed materials online and turn around hard copies in a day.

All of these tools, and more, make it possible for anyone to get an idea out of their head and into the world in a matter of days. Now you have no excuse for not at least giving it a shot – what have you got to lose?

START FOR YOUR OWN REASONS

Starting a business can be whatever you want it to be. Some people start one as a way to get rich – and that's fine. But, for me, what's more exciting is the idea that you can start with a blank page and go on to create something wonderful; something that makes the world a different place. You may even create a product that ultimately will give enjoyment to hundreds of thousands of people.

It is also possible to use your business to further causes that you feel strongly about. You can use your packaging and advertising to protest about issues – in the way that The Body Shop protested about animal rights, for example. You can also use it as a way to raise funds for charities that matter to you, and hopefully the product you are selling can be sourced in an ethical way.

For me, starting a business has completely changed my life. Not only has it brought me the financial freedom to live my life however I want, it has also taken me on wonderful adventures to over 50 countries – I'm extremely grateful that, unlike many of my friends, I don't have to work every day in a job that I hate.

As well as being financially rewarding and a lot of fun, seeing my business grow from the first few jars I made in my grandmother's kitchen to thousands of them adorning the shelves of supermarkets has been massively satisfying. It still puts a smile on my face when I walk into a massive supermarket store and see some jars of my jam there – especially in a foreign country!

Whatever reason you decide to start a business, the most amazing feeling is the one that comes from knowing that a whole adventure, a career and an impact on the world can all develop from just one simple idea written down on a piece of paper.

FOCUS

Our lives are so noisy. Noisier than they've ever been before. The average person checks Facebook more than 20 times a day. We take in information all day long from the TV, radio, newspapers, billboards, tweets, posts, YouTube videos, memes, FourSquare, text messages, phone calls, Skype, instant messenger, email and regular old-fashioned mail, and then somehow we even have some time left over for real-life conversations with the people we live with, the people we work with and the people we love.

We seem to have lost the ability to stop and think deeply about one thing at a time. We take in hundreds of ideas from all over the place and, instead of questioning each of them, we just take in the ones that fit and ignore those that don't. We're swamped with so much information that our brains are over-loaded – we can barely think for ourselves any more.

And it doesn't appear that anyone wants to live in the present moment either; the here and the now. Nobody picks up the phone and says, 'Hey, what are you doing, fancy a coffee right now?' That would seem weird in the always-busy society that we have created. Collectively, we suffer from the illusion of having a plan. It is assumed that we're all busy right now. The moment is already taken. Today is already booked. Tomorrow is already booked too, so the here and now better just wait until next week.

We're constantly scanning hundreds of different information outlets, waiting for something to happen, waiting for our lives to happen, waiting for some stroke of luck that will make all of our dreams come true.

In our work, we often tend to get to the end of the day not really knowing what we have achieved – have you ever experienced that sinking feeling when you leave the office after sitting at your computer for ten hours and ask yourself, 'What the hell did I actually do today?'

We've completely lost the ability to focus all of our energy on doing one thing at a time. On doing a good job of one thing each day. Instead, we skim the surface of hundreds of ideas, hundreds of different tasks, not really doing the best we can at any of them and not fully achieving what we can with our lives.

What's worse is that, by not committing ourselves to any one thing, we don't really live, we just wait. People go to dinner parties and check their phone every five minutes. They go to parties and are always busy finding out what's happening some-place else. If they could just live in the moment a bit more, enjoy what they're doing at that exact second, life could be a lot more fulfilling and a lot more fun.

Something amazing happens when you start giving all of your attention to one thing at a time. Whether it's the conversations you're having, the ideas you are working on or the time you're spending with the people you love, if you give each moment your undivided attention, you get the best out of every situation and the best out of yourself.

Generally, we have so many options as to what we can spend our attention on that we end up being completely scatter-brained. There are so many things we can do that generally we just do nothing. Making a choice and a commitment to focus on one thing is often a step too far for us. Infinite choice has a paralysing effect on our minds; it's easier to decide to do nothing than to pick from an infinite number of choices.

People tend to get very little work done as a result of all this, and thus never truly fulfil themselves. I meet a lot of people who – paralysed by the limitless opportunities for work that our globalised, digitised world provides – have no idea what to do with their lives.

There used to be a time when most decisions were made for you – you'd work in the local mill or factory and live the same life as your parents and pretty well everyone else around you. But now, the choice of what to do with your life is completely up to you.

In this book, I want to show what can happen in just 48 hours of undivided attention. By focusing all of my energy on working on one simple idea for two days, it's amazing how much ground can be covered. If we remove the constant interruptions of phone calls and Facebook updates from our lives, we can begin to work on tasks more deeply, enjoy our lives more, and have experiences with the people around us that are more meaningful.

The *48-Hour Start-Up* is an experiment in focus. If you just devote all of your energy to a task that has a simple and clearly defined goal, you can achieve in days what you previously thought would take years. If, instead, you try starting a business in the usual way, with all of the distractions that our modern lives bring, it may well indeed take you years.

PIZZA PILGRIMS

How to make a living out of doing something that you love

Almost everyone loves pizzas, so to make a living out of selling them is probably a dream that many people have. But given that there are probably more pizzerias in the world than any other type of restaurant, it surely takes a bit of guts to set out to start another one in what is undoubtedly a fairly crowded market.

Undeterred, brothers James and Thom Elliot decided to go on their 'pizza pilgrimage' to Italy, buying a vintage Ape van and driving it back to London. They picked up recipes and inspiration for their restaurant along the way and now, several years later, find themselves running a small chain of pizzerias in London that has developed something of a cult following.

Their story certainly sounds romantic, and they're definitely a couple of guys who are doing something that they love. But I know for sure that starting a business, especially a restaurant business, isn't all romance and fun. When I caught up with them recently for our podcast show, they reflected on conversations they have had with some of their friends – friends who are maybe working in corporate jobs in their thirties and bored out of their minds.

'Spending your twenties finding something that you love and are awesome at is the key.' But they warn that you shouldn't trick yourself into thinking that starting a business is going to be amazing every day and that you're going to skip off to work each morning as though you're in a Disney movie. What they can guarantee is that every day is going to be different. If you have a bad day, there's nothing to say that the next day isn't going to be amazing.

'Don't start a company because you want to have an easy life or because you think every day is going to be the best day of your life.' Running your own business is an amazingly varied and totally at-your-control-type lifestyle, and that's what these guys love about it.

'When you work for a big company, it's kind of like having emotional training wheels on – your best day is kinda great and your worst day is kinda bad. But when you work for yourself, your best day is kind of *Shawshank Redemption* rain-in-your-face amazing and the worst day is, well, really tough.'

On the topic of whether it helps to have a business partner with whom to share all of this emotional turmoil, they propose that it definitely does. 'We've found that having a business partner has made the highs even higher and has meant that when we do have lows there's someone there to get you through.'

You can listen to the full interview on the *48-Hour Start-Up* podcast show at 48hourstartup.org.

CHAPTER 2

COMING UP WITH AN IDEA

'How can I possibly come up with a good idea?
Surely all the good ones are already taken?'

Every business begins with an idea, so the first step in the 48-hour start-up process is to come up with one. Usually, this is where people fall into a great black hole of endless dreaming and scheming. Some people can't come up with any ideas at all and some come up with too many and can't decide which one to pick.

One of my all-time favourite quotes comes from an American called Charles H. Duell. All the way back in 1899, when he was the US Commissioner of Patents, he proposed that the Patent Office's days were numbered and that it ought soon to face closure. He proclaimed that *'Everything that can be invented, has been invented.'*

Of course, more than 100 years later, his comment strikes us as farcical. When we think of all of the innovation and change that has happened in the century that followed his proclamation, it is clear that he was very much wide of the mark. But the funny thing is that this is exactly the type of comment I hear people making almost every day.

If you watch programmes like *Dragons' Den* (or the US version, *Shark Tank*), you can easily be given the impression that the qualification for a good idea is that it is unique, that it is hitherto something that didn't exist in the world. On these TV shows, eccentric and hopeful inventors unpack a suitcase inside which they have carried some kind of bizarre contraption – like a special mop that cleans underneath the fridge or a gadget for de-icing your car windscreen in seconds.

Of course, these spectacles make for great television, but they don't actually tell the full story of what is and isn't a good idea. It is true that these hapless innovators are often quite correct when they say that their creation 'has never been done before' – but, sadly, there's often a reason for why that's the case!

What I have found in my career is that your idea doesn't necessarily need to be high-tech – although, of course, a lot of brilliant ideas are. A good idea definitely doesn't have to reinvent the wheel. What my experiences show is that it's possible to make something extraordinary out of something as ordinary as jam, beer or coffee.

USP IS DEAD

TV entrepreneurship shows probably also give you the impression that good ideas ought to have a patent. They bleat on about how important it is to 'protect' your idea. 'If you don't have a patent, someone else can just come along and steal your idea!' the 'dragons' shout as they shoot down another under-prepared entrepreneur.

In the real world, almost no businesses have a patent. Their ideas simply aren't innovative enough to be granted any kind of special protection from competition. And even those who do hold these certificates of monopoly over their ideas aren't really protected from much in the real world. If their idea is any good, someone will come along and find a way around their patent or maybe even come up with a better solution to the problem altogether.

So if I'm telling you that there is no need for your idea to be unique, surely this flies in the face of the conventional business mantra that every business must have a 'unique selling point'. I don't know about you but this principle was drilled into my head in business studies as if it were a fact of life – that all businesses only exist because they are doing something 'unique'.

When you stop to analyse this, you quickly realise that it is ludicrous. There are basically no unique businesses, except perhaps a few privileged government monopolies. All businesses have close competitors, easy replacements, copycats and imitators. Even those who are doing something unique soon find their uniqueness eroded by other people's innovations. So how come any of them survive?

Well, the truth is that it isn't by being unique that businesses succeed. It's partly by just being a little bit different – a bit better, a bit cheaper or a bit faster. It is undeniably also about having the best business model. But more than anything it's about having a unique story, a unique brand.

Sure, when I came up with the idea of making jam 100 per cent from fruit, this was a pretty novel idea. But it wasn't completely unique. And, as I'm sure you can imagine, many people have copied our concept over the years. But the one thing that people couldn't copy was my story.

Now you might say, 'Hey, it's easy for you to say that – you had this cute story of you and your gran.' Well, it's nice of you to say so, but to be honest I'm sure you also have a great story. About why you've decided to start your business, perhaps; or about who you are and what you believe in. The simple fact that you are a unique person is part of what makes your business unique, no matter how ordinary or commoditised its products might be.

Look, if my dad had lost his job and started selling jam door to door in middle age, that would have been a story. And if my gran had started selling jam in her senior years, that would have been the best story of all. Whoever you are, there is some story you can tell, something you can say that makes your brand special.

By bearing this in mind, you can take some of the pressure off yourself to come up with something completely different. Your idea doesn't need to be unique, it just has to be authentic. It has to come from the heart and be something about which you are passionate. With this in mind, you can start to look at the world as full of opportunity – if you don't have to do something unique, you can do anything.

SAME PROBLEM, DIFFERENT SOLUTION

If one thing makes you aware of the opportunity to reinvent even the most everyday of items, it's travel. I've been fortunate enough to travel to over 50 countries over the past few years, partly with SuperJam and partly for my own adventures.

What you quickly realise when you start to travel is that so many of the things we consider to be expected or essential in our lives are in fact alien concepts to people who happen to live in other countries.

Take some of the most fundamental ideas we have in Western society; that a toilet should be like a seat, with a lid and a flush. Or that food should be eaten with a knife and fork, sitting at a table. Most countries in the world view these fundamental things differently. I've been to places where they eat with their right hands, with chopsticks, with a spoon and fork, or just with a fork. I've been to places where I wasn't even sure how to use the toilet, or indeed whether I wanted to, so primitive was its design. And I can tell you, this isn't a cultural one-way street – in Japan they think our toilets are barbaric and in India they think it's disgusting that we touch our food with our left hands.

When you realise that even the most fundamental ideas about how we should live can be called into question, you realise that it is possible to reinvent anything and everything. And someone will.

I like to imagine a person from 100 years in the future coming to visit us here today. There are some things they will no doubt be familiar with, like ring pulls on fizzy-drink cans or shoelaces. But they'll be amazed that we don't yet have so many things they take for granted. The only difference between now and then is that some entrepreneurs in the meantime will come up with new ideas and products and, cumulatively, they will change the world.

Hopefully by now, with all this talk of changing the world, I've convinced you that the world is full of opportunity; that things are only the way they are because someone else made them that way – and that you have just as much right to change them as they did. Your idea can be unique and transformative, but the chances are that it won't be, and that's okay too.

UNITED STATES OF GREAT IDEAS

If you do have the time to travel in search of a great business idea, almost certainly your best bet is to take a flight to California or New York; still today the world's epicentres of entrepreneurship. People literally travel from all around America and around the world to move to Brooklyn or to San Francisco, with an idea in their head and a MacBook under their arm.

Any time I've visited these places I've seen restaurant concepts, food products, apps and all kinds of things that I've figured could also work back home. And, no doubt, many of these American start-ups will make it across the pond to conquer Europe if someone here isn't quick enough to build their own version of the same concept.

If you look at many of the great entrepreneurial success stories in Europe – for instance Innocent Smoothies, Ryanair, Kwik-Fit and BrewDog – they took their inspiration, at least in part, from what they saw happening in the States. In California they really lead the way when it comes to healthy food, craft beer and even craft coffee. In all my business ideas I have taken at least some inspiration from what I've seen going on over there.

For whatever cultural and historical reasons, our American cousins make for great entrepreneurs. They don't seem to have the same fear of failure as we do and it would seem that they're born with a natural self-confidence that helps them put their best foot forward from the moment they're born.

Whatever kind of business you are in, check out the American blogs on that topic. Talk to some Americans. Sign up for the magazines that are available over there. Purposefully go looking for a good idea to bring back home.

You can usually assume that if you're working on a product, there's probably someone in America who has already sold a million of them. Rather than come up with your own way of doing things from a blank piece of paper, why not look at them as your free Research & Development department?

They may have spent years working on this idea, testing different business models and designs. What you see now is the outcome of that: an idea that has been refined and tuned to succeed commercially. Why do the hard work all over again when you can simply stand on their shoulders? Don't be afraid of copying something that works. Sure, do it in your own way, but don't feel there's anything shameful about remixing other people's work – DJs have been doing it forever.

BE SECOND, FIRST

One of the best pieces of advice in business someone has given me came from the Scottish entrepreneur Sir Tom Farmer, the founder of Kwik-Fit. He believes in the philosophy of being 'second, first'. And I think that this strategy of being a 'fast-follower', whether you are taking inspiration from a business at home or abroad, is a great one. The importance of being first to market, the so-called 'first mover advantage', is dead. It was an idea initially popularised in the 1980s: that the first player in a given market would have some kind of inherent advantage from being first.

Sure, there can be all kinds of advantages that come from this – the kudos, the media coverage, the 'head start' on the competition. But when you think of the bigger picture, you realise that this doesn't tell the whole story of what it means to go first.

A totally untested and new idea carries the most risk, and very few of those succeed – studies consistently show that more than half will fail, some will survive and a few will be a tearaway success.

When you look at the companies that were the second in a given market, their odds are dramatically better. Shane Snow, in his excellent book *Smartcuts*, believes that less than 10 per cent of these companies fail. Wow, that means that someone who starts second is maybe 75 per cent less likely to fail.

Think about it – the companies that go first are those pioneering spirits who head out into the hills in search of gold, digging as they go. Most of them won't find anything and some will – by which time they'll be exhausted from all of their earlier digs. The person who gets word of their find and comes running up the hillside with their shovel next is the one who really wins.

The smart thing to do then, surely, is to look carefully for the new ideas that are working, figure out what they're doing well and what they're doing badly, then make your own version as fast as you can. If you can be number two before number three comes along, that's the best chance of success.

The people who started first have probably blown all their money and energy on things that didn't work before they hit upon what does work. You, on the other hand, start from day one with a model that works, just by copying theirs.

Now this might sound mean, 'stealing other people's ideas', but the truth is that there is no such thing as an original idea.

Those people were no doubt inspired by someone else, who in turn was copying another idea. Sure, they might not see it that way, but of course it's the truth.

WHO TO COPY

So, just like at school, it's one thing to copy, so long as you copy the right person. If their answers are as dumb as yours, then you haven't much increased your chances of success.

What you really need to do is establish quickly whether or not a new business that you come across on a blog or in the press is actually working. Find a way of seeing past the hype and the marketing spin.

Coming up with your idea will, of course, be one of the defining decisions you make in this process. Which means that it is worth taking a methodical approach to coming up with an idea that has the best chance of succeeding. And that means finding a product for which there is definitely going to be customers.

A classic place to start is to find out what the general size of the market is. If you can get this kind of information from a credible source like Mintel or the *FT*, great. It should take seconds. Crudely put, if the market is tiny and not growing then it's pretty improbable you'll be able to make a business out of it – even a small business.

ACTIONABLE IDEAS

Maybe your dream, like mine, is to sell your product to a retailer. But, if you want to have your first customer by Monday morning, you're probably going to need a business model that is based on making sales directly, since convincing retailers to stock your product can be an extremely lengthy process (it will typically

take six to twelve months ̶ ̶
retailer for it to make it to the ̶ ̶

So, if you are creating a product, ̶
making it yourself in the beginning o ̶
you can pass on to a manufacturer once you ̶

Making your product yourself or delivering ̶
personally in the beginning can be a very rich learnin ̶
tunity. Only if you make the product yourself will you get a ̶
sense of what sort of process is involved – giving you an opportunity to come up with the best way of doing it.

Selling directly to your first customers, whether your business
is a physical product or not, will give you the perfect opportunity to learn about how best to sell it, right from the coalface.

The closer you are to your customer, the easier it is for you
to learn what they like and don't like about your product and to
continually make changes, allowing your concept to evolve very
quickly. Going into this process with a willingness to make
improvements along the way means that your product doesn't
need to be perfect from day one.

This is true for every kind of business. This book is particularly focused on creating a physical product to sell online, but the
principles are just as relevant to selling a service, a purely online
concept, a retail store or any other kind of business. And besides,
whatever type of business you start, it is definitely going to need
an online component nowadays.

At this point, it's also worth being clear for your own sake
whether the business you hope to start as part of this project is
one that you want to become your full-time career, a lifestyle
business on the side or something else. Of course, the expecta-
tions you have for this business will have an impact on which
ideas are viable and which are not, based on the amount of time
you have available to grow them.

from pitching your concept to a major

shelves). you should focus on either

taking pre-orders that

have one in place.

your service

oppor-

idea in your

each other in

, you can never

e time researching

exciting new busi-

countries and which

opportunity.

pic, let's say food, prob-

ably u   ideas is just to google 'this
year's food u   gest blogs on that topic and
it'll soon become a   ot and what's not.

It's a good practice to   urself abreast of the 'start-up' scene' around the world and you can do this really easily by reading mainstream blogs and magazines such as *The Next Web*, *TechCrunch*, *Fast Company*, *Wired*, *Springwise*, *Trendspotting*, *CoolHunting* and *PSFK*.

I also like to know what cool new food brands are starting up, and *The Die Line*, *Lovely Package* and (in the UK) *The Drum* and sometimes *The Grocer* are good places to look for clues as to what's hot right now.

To stay up to date with what's happening in the world of start-ups, I check on the websites of various incubators and accelerators (places where entrepreneurs are given funding, office space and mentoring to get their high-growth companies off to a flying start). Some of the leading ones to check out are *Y Combinator*, *Wayra*, *Seedcamp*, *Tech Stars*, *Launchbox*, *DreamIT Ventures*, *SeedRocket*, *AlphaLab*, *BootupLabs*, *Shotput Ventures*, *Capital Factory*, *500startups*, *StartupBootcamp* and dozens of others. They usually list all of the companies that they have invested in, which gives you a sense of which ideas investors are excited by and which markets might prove to be fertile spaces for you to grow your business. Even though you may not have any plans to raise investment for your business, it's helpful to understand what the 'smart money' is thinking.

By keeping your finger on the pulse, you'll not only find ideas from other countries that you can simply adapt for your own market, but also the good ideas you come across will help to spark original ideas of your own. You might unearth a business model that you think could work for another product, for example.

YOUR INTERESTS

To me, a perhaps glaringly obvious way to start looking for ideas is to write a list of all the things you are interested in, everything that you think is exciting and fun to do.

By starting a business in a field that you're already passionate about, you'd be amazed at how much useful information you've absorbed about that topic already.

Having some background knowledge will be extremely valuable, since the best way to come up with a good idea is to come up with something that you can honestly say you'd buy yourself. If you don't think you'd buy it, it is patronising to think any customer out there would buy it either; they're just as smart as you.

As well as being interested in a topic, it helps if you have some kind of ability in that field! Of course there's nobody stopping you from learning a whole new skill if your dream is to do something totally out of your comfort zone, but that takes time.

Sometimes it's difficult to figure out what you're good at – quite often it's only a small part of what you do in your work. Our days are typically made up of a few things we're great at and lots of things we're just okay at.

Everyone has different abilities, and a good way to reflect on what yours are is to consider the things you find easy but that people around you think are difficult.

⏱ Day 1, 8am

In my case, I wrote a pretty long and random list of things that, off the top of my head, I thought were cool or that I am passionate about:

- Start-ups
- Campervans
- Road trips
- Vegan food
- Animal rights
- Travel
- Comedy
- Cookbooks
- Food trucks
- Ice-cream vans
- Tiny houses
- Simple living
- Growing vegetables
- My dog
- Learning languages
- Self-improvement
- The elderly
- Travel writing
- Life hacks
- Productivity apps
- Design
- Crafts
- Making things
- Liquorice
- Inventors
- Simple electronics
- Breakfast
- Children's books
- Documentaries
- Chocolate
- Tea
- Coffee
- Porridge
- Adventure travel

From that list, I picked out a few that I was particularly passionate about or interested in and wrote down what it was that, in a nutshell, made me interested in the first place. These were topics that I had a gut feeling would have some potential for a business, given that they are niche interests that people are willing to spend a lot of money on.

Articulating why I like them in this way may seem a little strange, but it's a good way of getting to the heart of what's special about these topics – the reason why I care about them:

- Vegan food: I feel strongly about animal cruelty and want to eat healthily.
- Adventure travel: I love having 'authentic' experiences in foreign countries.
- Ice-cream vans: I love when they stop on our street – they seem to me to be a timeless embodiment of fun and simple pleasure.
- Porridge: I like a wholesome breakfast at the start of the day and like to 'pimp' my oats with fruit, chocolate, nuts and seeds.

Scribble down your own ideas in a notebook.

PROBLEMS

Day 1, 8.20am

A perfect place to start in coming up with an idea is to identify the problems with your chosen themes. If *you* are having those problems, no doubt other people are too; and if you can honestly say you would be willing to pay money to solve those problems, the chances are you're not alone.

Vegetarian food
- Poor selection of vegetarian/vegan food in supermarkets
- Lack of exciting recipes
- Can become boring over time
- Don't know many other vegetarians/vegans

Adventure travel

- Can take a lot of time to research where to go
- Unable to speak foreign languages
- Guidebooks only offer 'the sights'
- Locals try to rip you off

Ice-cream vans

- Hard to find an ice-cream van when you want one!
- They don't have anything to do when it's not sunny
- The quality is usually pretty bad
- No dairy free or healthier options

Porridge

- Supermarket oats are boringly plain
- Branded oats are frighteningly full of sugar
- Don't usually have time to pimp my porridge

Scribble down your own ideas in a notebook.

BUSINESS MODELS

With a long list of problems, we now have somewhere to aim our creative energy. But, rather than just coming up with solutions for these problems out of the blue, it is best if we try to come up with them in conjunction with a business model that might make our solution a profitable one.

Coming up with a solution to a problem is one thing, coming up with a business is something else entirely. Attaching your solution to a business model is what makes the difference.

There are hundreds of different business models you can employ. Below are a few, but you will have a list of your own based on which ones you think have the most potential.

Advertising: If you can create a site, a magazine or an app that draws enough traffic, you can generate revenue using the likes of Google AdSense, earning a few pennies every time one of your visitors clicks on an advertiser's link. The more targeted your site is to a particular segment, the more valuable the ad space will be. Some topics will be more valuable to advertisers; finance, gambling, utilities, mobile phone companies and other big-ticket items will pay well for clicks.

Agency: If you have good connections within a particular field, you can create a site that lists all of the 'experts' whom you have access to for clients to book. You could start an agency for DJs, medical lecturers, chefs or cocktail waiters for parties.

Affiliate: By linking to companies that offer products and services relevant to your users, you can earn a commission on any money they spend with those stores. This model works especially well if, for example, you create content about holidays or financial products; the commissions can be significant.

Concierge: Some things are just so messy and complicated that people are willing to pay someone in the know to deal with them – this works especially well for travel, for private parties or for household maintenance.

Daily deals: There has been a massive proliferation of Groupon-type sites over the past few years, very few of them making any money. However, perhaps if you can apply the model to your own particular niche and build up a large enough database of email subscribers, you could build a business.

Digital downloads: If you can create a digital product – for example, a book, an educational course, music, film, software or font – you can sell it as a digital download either on your own site or through Amazon, Apple and other places, and deliver it to your customers with no cost. Once you've done the work of creating it, you're making 100 per cent profit on every sale.

Door to door: I couldn't write this section without mentioning the business model that gave me my own start in business. There's absolutely nothing stopping you from knocking on doors, offering your product directly to your target consumers. Although this is a very grassroots way of doing things, the cost of getting started is very low and the market feedback couldn't be any more direct. Around the world, there are some huge companies that started with a lone entrepreneur walking up and down streets plying their wares to anyone who would listen.

Drop shipping: This is where you set up an online store and, rather than holding stock yourself, just send an order to the manufacturer, who ships it straight to your customer. You take a cut of what the customer paid you before paying the manufacturer the trade price of the item.

Ecommerce: Probably the simplest business model is to source or make a product yourself and then sell it online through your site.

Freemium: One of the most popular models on the internet is to offer a basic version of your service for free, all the time encouraging customers to upgrade to a premium version that contains extra benefits.

Live events: A site can be a great way to sign up customers for real-world events, such as cupcake decorating classes, secret dinners in your own home or puppy-training classes.

Manufacturing: Good old-fashioned 'making stuff'. I got my start by making a product in my parents' kitchen and there's nothing to say that you couldn't do the same. Perhaps you can make something by hand yourself, then one day you can graduate to factory production.

Marketplace: It is extremely hard to build a successful marketplace, such as eBay or Airbnb, because you need to attract a critical mass of both buyers and sellers. However, that's not to say there aren't opportunities to create marketplaces for all kinds of things: dog walkers, cleaners, graphic designers or private parking spaces, perhaps.

Matchmaker: This is where you have lots of people looking for the same thing and your job is to put them together. The classic matchmaker is of course for dating, but it could apply equally for people who want a holiday companion, who want to swap homes over the holidays, or maybe want to join a book group in their area.

Mobile apps: Build an iPhone/Android app and either give it away free (with an option inside the app to buy additional features or in-app advertising) or sell it for a one-off price or a monthly recurring payment.

Party planning: A seemingly redundant business model in the digital age, the idea of 'direct selling' your product person-to-person may seem a little unusual, but it can be extremely successful. Companies such as Tupperware pioneered the model of setting up parties where local reps – small-scale entrepreneurs in their own rights – would demonstrate and sell their products to their network. In recent times, this model has been reinvented to sell wine, beauty products, cookware and all sorts of things.

Pay what you want: Some people have experimented with letting consumers set their own price, which works especially well for things like digital products, where it doesn't matter if some people choose to pay only a few pennies.

Peer-to-peer: A good peer-to-peer site is hard to create, because you are completely reliant on the willingness of complete strangers to share with each other. However, a good example is course-note sharing sites – where you can pay a small fee (or upload work of your own) to access other people's academic essays. You could apply the same model to recipes, travel reviews or betting tips, for example.

Pop-up store: If your dream is to open a retail store, an ideal way to test out the waters is by opening an outlet for a short period of time. There are online marketplaces that you can use to book quirky, high-footfall sites to enable you to offer your products for sale to the general public, sometimes even in high-footfall locations.

Pre-sales: Especially with product design, a lot of entrepreneurs are encouraging their customers to buy before anything is actually produced at all. This has been particularly popular with Kickstarter campaigns, where the business only manufactures their product if enough people commit to buying it, so they know they're onto a winner straight off the bat.

Production on demand: It's really cool that you can design a product, promote it for sale online and only press 'go' on production once someone places an order. This eliminates the risk of holding stock that maybe nobody will want to buy. If you're sourcing from the Far East, you'll need to make it clear to people how long they may have to wait before receiving their order.

'Razor and blades': If you can get customers to invest in a relatively inexpensive machine (like a printer or a coffee machine) that requires ongoing consumables, you potentially have a very profitable business in the long run.

Retail product: You may well take the route of creating a product, finding a third-party manufacturer and using your site simply as a way to promote it to retailers and consumers, selling your brand through bricks-and-mortar retailers.

Self-publishing: The internet has made it very easy for anyone to get their ideas out there. Some people have built a business on the back of publishing their own work – whether that's music, books or podcasts. If you have a creative idea, you can usually find and learn how to use the tools you need relatively easily.

Social network: Starting a social network probably isn't a great idea, given the fairly well-established companies that have achieved success in this arena. Having said this, you may well be able to create a network around a very specific interest. It is important to combine online with offline by having real-world events, supported by a website where people can sign up.

Software as a service: Create a piece of software and, rather than selling it as a one-off purchase, charge users a monthly fee.

Subscription: There are hundreds of subscription services popping up all the time and they're almost a cliché on the start-up scene; 'stick something in a box and charge a subscription'. But the truth is that, if what you're offering is worthwhile, your customers will remain loyal, earning you a predictable income stream.

THE IDEA

(🕐) Day 1, 8.32am

The next step is to try to solve some of the problems you've identified using one or more of the business models that appeal to you. To give you an idea of how simple this can be, below are all of the ideas that I came up with. For some of the problems I identified, I simply couldn't come up with any solutions at all, which is probably always going to be the case.

Vegan food

Problem:
- Poor selection of vegan food in supermarkets

Solutions:
- Ecommerce site selling vegan food online
- Subscription selling a monthly selection of vegan foods

Problem:
- Lack of exciting recipes

Solutions:
- Peer-to-peer vegan-recipe-sharing site
- Vegan-recipe app
- Deliver a weekly subscription box of ingredients and recipes for vegan meals

Problems:
- Can become boring over time
- Don't know many other vegans

Solutions:
- Live events; meet-ups for vegans with speakers and food
- Social network for vegans
- Vegan matchmaking dating site

Adventure travel

Problem:
- Can take a lot of time to research where to go

Solutions:
- Concierge service for unusual travel wishes
- 'Off the beaten path' travel packages agency

Problem:
- Unable to speak foreign languages

Solutions:
- Online foreign-language tutor marketplace
- Agency for local tour guides and interpreters

Problem:
- Guidebooks only offer 'the sights'

Solution:
- An alternative travel guide and blog, with advertising and affiliates

Problem:
- Locals try to rip you off

Solution:
- Toughen up!

Ice-cream vans

Problem:
- Poor quality and unhealthy product

Solution:
- Pop-up healthy, luxury ice-cream van concept

Problem:
- Hard to find an ice-cream van when you want one!

Solution:
- An app that orders an ice-cream delivery

Porridge oats

Problem:
- Supermarket oats are boringly plain

Solution:
- A retail product: super-luxury, pre-pimped oat-mix tubs, with dried fruit, chocolate chips, seeds and spices

Problem:
  • Branded oats are frighteningly full of sugar

Solution:
  • A self-published recipe book, sharing my amazing porridge recipes

Problem:
  • Don't usually have time to pimp my porridge

Solution:
  • A pop-up store selling pimped-up porridge pots to take away

Scribble down your own ideas in a notebook.

Having gone through this process, coming up with a range of concepts of variable quality, there are a couple on my list that sound like they could be feasible businesses. Most importantly, they sort of excite me and would be things I can imagine paying for myself.

I like the idea of a vegan subscription box because I can very much see how I'd go about starting it. I do have a little experience with other subscription businesses, so that would certainly help.

An online foreign-language tutor marketplace also sounds like a terrific idea. I'd love to be able to hire a tutor by the hour to teach me Korean and help make my appearances on Korean home TV shopping a little more cohesive!

I also love the idea of selling pre-mixed porridge oats. Maybe it's because it's breakfast time on my first day of this process, but I have a feeling that this could be a good product.

The above are all topics I can imagine other people would be interested in, too. I can certainly picture lots of people searching on Google for these things, which is really important, as that will be an important source of customers for any online business.

If people aren't searching for your product, it's hard to imagine they'll ever stumble across it. In my opinion, it's much easier to sell people something they want and are searching for than to try to sell them something they had no idea they wanted.

So now for the task of deciding between these three potentially valid ideas. I don't know much about foreign-language tuition and can't imagine how exactly I would build a market-place site in just one weekend, so let's scrap that one.

Food happens to be something of a passion of mine so both of the other ideas seem a lot more appealing. To help decide between the two, I head for Google and type: '2016 food trends'. The first article that comes up lists, at number-one spot no less, 'oatmeal' – the American name for porridge. It seems that I could be on to something.

Day 1, 9.13am

Porridge, 1. Vegan subscription boxes, 0.

I decide to take a look at the market size. I quickly search for 'UK porridge oats market size' and a *Grocer* article puts it at £241m and growing fast. Sounds promising.

Finding similar stats on vegan foods is more challenging, so I try a different tack. I use a free service from Google called Google Trends, which allows you to see how the popularity of a given topic is changing over time.

Sure looks like porridge is outpacing vegan food, even though they're both growing well. What really jumps out is how popular porridge is in January, when people are trying to get healthy.

I decide to jump on my bicycle and do some quick market research. I head over to my local supermarket and check out what's going on in the world of oats. All kinds of things, as it turns out. Just as with every good idea, there are already people who are working on the idea of making premium porridge oats.

The oats in the supermarket range from 60p for a 1kg bag of supermarket own-brand oats, all the way up to £4 for some fancy oats with healthy ingredients.

Now, while I don't think it's important for my idea to be truly unique, I do think I'll need to do something sufficiently different to what's already there to be able to convince, in this case, the store owner to take the other products off the shelves and put mine there.

My gut feeling when I look at the shelves is that there is an opportunity to do something more exciting there. Nobody has tried to create a particularly original brand, with a sense of humour. And none of the flavours that I can see are particularly exciting. On closer inspection, most of the premium brands have added sugar.

Who knows if this idea will work or not, but I think it's worth a shot!

MY IDEA

After less than an hour of focused thinking and a bit of googling, I've come up with an idea that I think might stand a chance. I'm going to take the idea of 'pimped-up porridge oats' and run with it.

Is my idea any good?

⏱ Day 1, 9.32am

Let's be honest here, the idea that you have just come up with in an hour could well stink and you're just too sleepy to tell at this time in the morning. So I've come up with a quick checklist to help you decide whether your idea is worth trying or not.

A lot of people spend years agonising over whether or not their idea is good, so hopefully this makes it easier to figure out. Basically, if your idea doesn't pass this test, go back to step one and come up with something else. Don't be precious about your ideas – they're free! If your first one doesn't look promising, don't hold on to it as if it were a baby; just throw it away and come up with something else. You've just seen how quickly you can come up with new ideas if you put your mind to it!

Checklist of what makes a good idea:
- Are you interested in this product?
- Would you buy this product – honestly, would you?
- Do you know enough about this kind of business to stand a chance?
- Are enough other people as interested in this as you are to make a business?
- Is there a compelling story about why *you* are starting this business?
- Can you conceivably put a product into the world in 48 hours' time?
- Is the competition sufficiently rubbish that you think you can do better?
- Does it pass the grandma test?

So, let's put my 'pimped-up porridge oats' idea to the test.

Are you interested in this product?
Yes, I eat it as often as I can be bothered to make it! I'm also interested in healthy food in general and there's something exciting about making a traditional food like porridge modern and fun.

It's really important to work on something you find interesting. I can't stress this point enough. If all that excites you about it is the thought that it might make you some dough, not only is that a bit too Donald Trump for my taste, it's also a bad strategy.

The thing is, starting a business is really tough. You'll face all kinds of challenges that at the moment you can't quite picture. Only if you're working on a project that interests you will you be able to keep ploughing on in the face of those challenges. You do your best work when you're working on something that excites you, so it makes good business sense to start one doing something you love.

Would you buy this product – honestly, would you?

Yes, I would, so long as it tastes great. I'm usually too lazy to make porridge at all, but if there were a natural mix that has lots of different ingredients in it, I'd buy this rather than have to make it myself.

A lot of entrepreneurs rely on the false hope that their potential customers are stupid, that they'll fall for some kind of trick or be willing to pay over the odds for a product that they could happily buy from the supermarket for much less. Consumers are incredibly tough, way more savvy than you might hope, and they have absolutely no regard for your feelings or dreams.

If you wouldn't honestly buy your product yourself, knowing everything that you do about how it's made and what the alternatives to it are, then you certainly shouldn't expect anyone else to want to buy it. You absolutely have to be your harshest critic on this one.

Do you know enough about this kind of business to stand a chance?

Yes, in my case I probably have learned a few things about this particular business! I am no expert in oats specifically, so there could well be big gaps in my knowledge, but I do know lots about starting a food brand.

Now, at this point you might protest: hey, you're starting a business doing something you already understand! You've started a food business before, so isn't this cheating? Well, here's the thing. My advice to you also would be to do something you have experience of.

Are enough other people as interested in this as you are to make a business?
Yes, I know for a fact that oats are a big business. Breakfast cereal is huge. Are there enough people like me who would pay a premium for luxury porridge oats with added healthy ingredients? That remains to be proven, but my gut tells me so.

Now there's a temptation when coming up with ideas to come up with something so niche that only a few people will care about it. Try to avoid those ideas! Sure, they might pass questions 1 and 2 with flying colours, but that doesn't mean they should be turned into a business.

I like ideas that focus on mainstream product categories, or indeed a niche within those categories. I'm much less enthusiastic about ideas that solve problems that aren't really problems at all.

Some business books will tell you that you need to know what the size of the market is. I've seen plenty of entrepreneurs argue over whether the market for their type of product is £100m or £200m. In my book, so long as you choose something that is in a massive market, it doesn't really matter precisely how big it is.

Is there a compelling story about why you are starting this business?
Yes, the idea of selling oats fits nicely with my jam-selling background! Not only that, but oats are very healthy, which fits nicely with the values of SuperJam. Being from Scotland, there's also a good link and, aside from all of that, I think there's something fun about a young guy trying to make something old-fashioned like oats into something fun!

You might be wondering why it's important to have a story. 'What if I don't want to get publicity for my idea?' Well, having a story isn't just about getting into the papers; it's about having a compelling reason for why your customers should listen to you instead of the competition. What is it that makes you so special?

I can assure you that if you're working on something that truly interests you, that you truly would buy yourself, then probably there is a story in there. Maybe the story is about why you're so passionate about this, what the experience was that provoked you to think of this idea or any number of other things.

Later in the book we'll talk about how to tell your story, but for now it's a good idea to ask yourself whether you feel this idea authentically fits with you. Imagine someone asking, 'Why did *you* start this business?' and if it feels as though there's an authentic reason, then it's all good. If it feels that this idea doesn't actually fit with your values or your background, then maybe other people will see that too and it'll hinder your chances of success.

Can you conceivably put a product into the world in 48 hours' time?
Yes, I can totally imagine that if I put my mind to it I can use some of my home porridge recipes to create a range of, say, three mixes. I can get some off-the-shelf packaging, create a simple brand and find somewhere to sell the first few dozen two days from now.

There's no golden rule that says you have to start a business within two days and, indeed, this process may well take you a little longer; that's okay. But if your idea is so complicated that you can't see how you would make a basic version of it within a short space of time, then maybe it's also too complicated for you to get around to starting.

The point isn't to create the absolute perfect version of your idea. It's to create a simple but good version, something that you can get onto the market and then make changes to it as you learn what people really want.

If it seems impossible to start something quickly, maybe think of ways to simplify the first version of your product. For instance, if your idea is to start a restaurant, why not run a pop-up supper club in your house? Or rent a food truck to test out your recipes and build a following before making the leap to bricks and mortar?

If your idea is to sell your product to a big retailer, maybe try selling it at a market first. Or if you want to create an online service, try using off-the-shelf software to get a basic version of your idea to market, learning what people really want and then building something from scratch afterwards, safe in the knowledge that what you are spending thousands to build is exactly what people want.

Is the competition sufficiently rubbish that you think you can do better?
Without insulting any of them, I do think I could do something better at the premium end of the market. There are a couple of innovative start-ups with good packaging and products that suit their particular target market well. There are also some massive players, like PepsiCo's Quaker Oats, swimming in the same pond. Thankfully, though, it is a big pond and there's space for a brand with a sense of fun to swim alongside them.

As you can see, I have chosen a market where there is lots of competition. There are some huge companies. I even have friends who sell products in this market and I come across new breakfast cereal start-ups all the time, so I know it's not an open field.

Surely this goes against everything we're taught? That you have to go to a place where there are no big companies to compete against? Well, yes, it would be wonderful if there were markets that don't have any competition, but that just isn't reality.

If you can, however, find a market that is dominated by brands that are big but not lovable, that's a great place to go. Being a small player, a challenger, a 'David vs Goliath', is your golden ticket against these monolithic corporations that nobody really likes.

Big companies are a little slow to react to new players, partly out of complacency but also because it takes them longer to do things. It certainly takes a big company more than 48 hours to launch a new product! They also often don't have an authentic story like you do – so you should always use your authenticity and your story as your magic weapon.

So, even though there is competition in the oat world, I don't see many brands that have a cult following. There are no super-stars. Because of this, I think the competition is crappy enough that I might just stand a chance.

If you're not quite so fortunate and instead find yourself trying to compete against superstars, that's when you need to reconsider your idea. If your plan is to go head to head with Amazon or Apple or with a well-funded, beautifully designed, hardworking start-up, then I'd try something else. Life's too short to try to compete with smart companies when there's plenty of ordinary, and even dumb, companies you can compete against instead.

Does it pass the grandma test?

At this point I'd like to introduce you to one of the most impor-tant tests you can do on a business concept: the grandma test. No matter how high-tech or complicated your innovation is, no matter how much detail you've had to go into to solve it, if you can't explain it to your grandma, or any grandma for that matter, you haven't thought it through enough.

Now this isn't to say that grandmas aren't smart; quite the contrary. Mine is very smart indeed. She understands what Google is – she doesn't understand how it works, and neither do most people, but she understands what it does and why you'd want to use it.

If I can successfully sell my grandma on the idea of Google search, one of the most high-tech products on the planet, you'd better be able to sell her on yours, because I'm guessing it's something less ground-breaking.

So, it's time to run the grandma test on my porridge idea. Over a quick cuppa, I casually pitch my idea to her.

I talk about how I'm working on launching a new product after her jam recipe went down so well. 'You haven't come here to steal my other recipes, have you?' she jokes.

'No, don't worry, there's no need to call your intellectual property lawyer,' I joke. 'But I would love to know what you think of my new idea.'

I explain that I've figured that porridge seemed like a good place to start. I want to make oats more exciting for people who, maybe, find the traditional Scottish way of eating them with just a pinch of salt a little, er, boring.

It turns out that she actually puts banana in her porridge so she's totally into the idea of pimping her oats. I explain that I'm going to sell pre-mixed packs of oats with dried fruit, nuts, seeds, chocolate chips, that sort of thing.

'Sounds lovely.'

We're on.

⏱ Day 1, 9:52am

BOOMF.COM – INSTAGRAM MARSHMALLOWS

How to come up with an original idea

As part of the *48-Hour Start-Up* podcast series, I interviewed one of the most original entrepreneurs that I have ever met: Andy Bell, the co-founder of the internet marshmallow company, Boomf.com, which you may well have seen advertised on TV.

He's a serial entrepreneur who finds it easy to come up with original business ideas – such as a pocket-sized Instagram photo projector and personalised bath salts. I wanted to ask him for a few tips that might help generate some great ideas.

On whether or not your idea needs to be truly unique, Andy reassures me that there is a huge range of possibilities. He suggests that actually most businesses compete on execution rather than pure originality, so you shouldn't really worry about doing something completely new.

If you're struggling to come up with an idea at all, he suggests that you work on a topic you already know something about and that you should be fairly regimented about your idea-generation. Just force yourself to come up with a large number of ideas, ideally with the help of other people, family or friends perhaps, and be willing to scrap the ones that are rubbish. Through this process, you'll uncover some gems more easily than trying to tease out that single 'eureka' moment.

Thankfully, like myself, Andy is a fan of just getting your product to market rather than agonising over whether or not it's perfect:

> How to validate whether or not your idea is any good is something we talk about a lot and, particularly in the internet world, there's so much enthusiasm for testing and minimum viable products. But, I think, particularly with consumer products, that it's so hard to get any sense of what will work, until it's real.

He also believes in not keeping your ideas to yourself:

> Share your idea with anyone who'll listen – it's far more likely to propagate or mutate in an interesting direction. There's just so many more ideas to talk about than there are people to implement them.

You can listen to the full interview on the *48-Hour Start-Up* podcast show at 48hourstartup.org.

CHAPTER 3

A JOURNEY OF A
THOUSAND MILES ...

... starts with just a single step, as the saying goes. Or perhaps a couple of dozen steps in the case of a 48-hour start-up. Now that we have a more refined version of our idea, ready to put into action, this is a good time to write a complete list of tasks that need to be completed over the remaining day and a half.

Building a business in such a short time might well seem overwhelming, but once you break down the entire process into a couple of dozen tiny steps, it suddenly starts to feel very possible.

There are some online applications that you might find help-ful for managing your to-do lists for this project, and indeed in general, such as Evernote, TeuxDeux, Mindjet and Flow. Or, much more likely, you can just grab a pen and paper and write a list of the steps that you imagine you need to take to go from having your idea in your head to having a product ready to sell.

TO-DO LIST

Day 1, 10.10am

Of course, your list will be different to mine, but here are the steps that I plan to complete in the next couple of days to get my product to market. And just for the satisfaction of it, I've crossed out the tasks that I've already done.

Day 1:

Already done:
- ~~Write down my interests.~~
- ~~Identify problems with these things.~~
- ~~Brainstorm possible solutions.~~
- ~~Match solutions to business models.~~
- ~~Select the ideas that seem feasible.~~
- ~~Pick the idea that has the best chance of success.~~
- ~~Run the grandma test~~

Still to do:
- Talk to a customer.
- Research the competition's pricing.
- Decide my price and figure out if it's possible.
- Check I wouldn't need to sell an insane volume to cover fixed costs.
- Sense-check the idea with an expert.
- Come up with a name.
- Create a strapline.
- Register a domain name.
- Set up a company email address.
- Register a phone number.
- Find a designer to create the brand and packaging.
- Create a mood board.
- Choose possible fonts.
- Brief designer to create logo and branding.
- Source the product.
- Order off-the-shelf packaging for the first batch of product.
- Order promotional materials.
- Find food stylist and photographer to shoot my product.
- Write the basic text and info for the packaging and website.
- Zzzzzzzzzzzzzzzzzz: time to catch some sleep!

Day 2:

- Print the label designs at a print shop, attach to packaging.
- Get the food stylist to shoot the product.
- Build the website.
- Create social media accounts.
- Upload the final product images to the website.
- Figure out how to get the first customers.
- Send out the first order!

When I break the process down into these simple steps, it seems totally feasible, even given the tight timeframe. There's a lot to do but there are quick and easy ways to do each of these steps and I'll share how I do each of them as we go through the book.

TALK TO A CUSTOMER

This step is so blatantly simple and so easy that it is often overlooked. In all companies, we develop really abstract ideas of who our customers are and what it is they want. We read studies about them and market research reports and read up on the latest trends. Sometimes, though, the best answers can be found by simply talking to our customers and listening to what they say.

Now, Steve Jobs famously said that his customers didn't know what they wanted until he showed it to them. I think it's true that people don't really know what they want; I certainly don't. So just asking people straight up what they want is not going to give you useful information.

However, you can learn a lot from what people actually do. Which of your competitors' products do they buy and why? Where did they first hear about that brand? Where do they buy it from? What do they do with it? What problems do they have with it? That sort of stuff.

The kind of questions you ask will be dependent on what kind of product you are selling. Particularly if you are trying to sell to businesses, there is a huge amount of value in understanding how they already solve the problem you are working on and what about it still causes them pain.

The first step is going to be finding a customer, or a few customers, to talk to. In my case, since my product will be selling through stores, it makes sense to try getting in touch with a retail buyer to ask what it would take for them to put something like this onto their shelves.

ASK A BUYER

When I was originally trying to sell SuperJam to Waitrose and I showed up at 16 years old wearing my dad's suit, I received what was probably the most useful advice of my whole career. All I had was an idea, I didn't really know how to put it into action, and sitting across a table from me was someone who could tell me how to do it.

Sometimes, when people are trying to sell their product to a retailer, especially a big one, they think that the only approach is to go there and pretend they have all the answers, with all guns blazing, *The Apprentice* style. In fact, if you can just be honest with the buyer, tell them what you're trying to achieve and why, you'd be amazed at how willing they will be to give you some advice.

Whatever kind of customer you're trying to sell to, the most important thing for you to do is actually listen. Be willing completely to change your concept in light of what customers say. If everyone tells you it needs to be blue, then it needs to be blue.

So many entrepreneurs are totally pig-headed about their idea – they just listen to the information that strengthens their case, ignoring whatever presents a challenge to their concept. Quite often they don't even ask anyone what they think of it, so cocksure are they that their idea is perfect just the way it is. Having the humility simply to ask other people for advice is probably the number-one way of increasing the speed at which you can develop fantastic products.

When I went through the process of getting feedback from the Waitrose buyer, he told me everything I was doing was wrong – the labels, the recipes, the price. But he did say that, in general, my idea of 100 per cent fruit jam was a good one. With his encouragement, I went back to the drawing board and gave everything another shot.

Working with a designer, I created a set of labels, found a factory to work with me and came up with a new range of flavours. Unfortunately, when I presented these ideas to the buyer, he explained that the labels we created were too silly, the factory I had chosen was too expensive and he didn't even like the flavours I had made – so basically everything had to be thrown in the bin and I started all over again.

Even though I was deflated, the buyer told me that I still had a good idea – he gave me advice about what my packaging design needed to achieve, what our pricing needed to be and what sort of flavours he thought would work best.

So when I did finally go back to him for a third time, having listened to everything he said, it was pretty hard for him to say no. He had become so involved in the process of developing the idea that in some ways it probably became his baby too. Of course, that wouldn't have been the case if I'd just ignored his feedback.

As for my oats business, it's probably not practical to imagine that I will be able to lift up the phone to the Tesco breakfast cereals buyer and pick their brains about it. But there are certainly lots of people I can talk to very easily who can help to give me a steer on how to develop my product so that it would appeal to them.

At this point, you should have absolutely no fear of being bold enough just to ask a potential customer what they think of your idea. For me, the opportunity is right around the corner, in the form of the local independent grocery store.

⏱ Day 1, 10.22am

I head around there right away, and buy a few groceries so that I don't feel guilty about wasting their time asking for advice. As I'm at the checkout I ask the man serving me how his weekend was and use our casual conversation as an opportunity to tell him a bit about what I'm up to.

'At the moment I'm working on creating a new premium porridge brand. Maybe you'd have some thoughts on it actually; looks like you already sell a few here. Do you find they're popular?' Turns out he has a bit of an interest in porridge oats himself and he invites me over to where they are stocked in the store so we can talk further about them. He's actually quite enjoying being asked his opinion at this point.

'Now, what you want to do is make sure that the packaging is really good. Something eye-catching. Don't go for a bag; those just look so messy on the shelves and when they burst it's a total nightmare.'

I ask him whether, if I was to come back tomorrow with a couple of cases of product, with eye-catching packaging and not in a bag, he'd try them out on his shelves. 'Tomorrow? You're going to come back here tomorrow with a product?' he asks, wondering what on earth is going on. Not entirely sure if I am joking or not, he agrees.

'Okay, it's a deal.'

CALL A CUSTOMER

What you're trying to sell will determine how you can contact potential customers. One method that I have used in the past is to get hold of contact numbers of people who have opted in to marketing calls and simply ring them up.

You can buy databases online of all sorts of groups of consumers; for example, those who have bought a new car in the past six months or those who own a dog. You'll be amazed at how easy it is and it'll probably make you a little warier about how widely you share your own data.

A quick Google search will reveal hundreds of consumer data companies, all eager to sell you a database of prospects' phone numbers, email and home addresses. Of course, you need to be sure that the agency you are buying the data from has acquired people's contact details ethically – each person must have opted in to allow third parties to contact them.

You really only need about 50 contacts, so you should negotiate to get these for free as a trial. Tell the agency that you just want to run a small test of the quality of their data, with the intention of buying a larger dataset once your business is up and running (which you may well decide to do, so I'm not telling you to lie). In most cases, they will be happy to send you this data for free.

Now's the part that nobody likes doing – picking up the phone. Just give people a ring and ask politely if they'd mind helping you with a new business idea that you're working on. If you use the word 'help', you'll be amazed at how forthcoming people are with their ideas and suggestions – it is human nature to be willing to help someone else, especially if you sound friendly.

If you are embarrassed by the idea of wasting strangers' time with your market research survey, you could offer them one of your products for free when you launch, or let them know that you will stick their name into a free prize draw.

I once spent about six months trying to launch a healthy food delivery company for older people. Imaginatively enough, I was planning on calling it SuperMeals. To get some handle on what older people liked and didn't like, I bought a database of customers who had previously bought from one of the competitor companies and who had opted in to hear about other 'meals on wheels' services. Perfect.

I spent an afternoon calling up pensioners and asking if they'd mind letting me know how they got on with their previous 'meals on wheels' supplier. They were so happy to have someone listen to their feedback and I learned more about my potential customers from that than from the many volumes of press articles, market research reports and other abstracted opinions that I worked my way through.

In the end, that particular business idea was scrapped, partly because I learned from these customers just how complicated their individual needs were. Every person I spoke to had different dietary requirements, making a meal delivery service extremely complicated to set up. More than anything, I quickly grasped that my gut feeling of what would be an acceptable price for a product like that was way out of line. These were people living on a pension, who had to look after every penny.

I tell you this story because I want you to know that it's okay to drop your idea. If, when you talk to customers, you realise that everything you assumed was wrong beyond the possibility of redemption, you can scrunch it up, throw it in the bin and try something else. It's not a big deal.

When you do talk to your potential customers, whether you decide to call them or meet them in person, here are a few key things that you are trying to find out at this stage:

What do they think of your idea?

You need to make sure that they feel totally able to give you honest feedback – tell them that you are looking for the flaws in your idea; that way they feel they're helping you when they point them out. It doesn't feel good to criticise someone's ideas, even if they are a complete stranger, so you might actively need to encourage them to do so.

You can ask them things like, if they were in your shoes, what would they do to create a great product in this market?

What would they expect from your product?

It's really good to get a sense of what would be important to consumers if they bought your product – what are the 'sacred cows'? These are things that absolutely, under any circumstance, your product has to be able to do. Their answers might flag up some super-detailed criteria that you would otherwise not have thought about: the packaging can't be more than 20cm high or the product won't fit on the shelf, for example. Without such information, you could easily develop a product, only to find out at the final hurdle that it's just too big to fit on the shelf, or that there's some other equally banal problem.

What other types of products do they buy?

Find out which of your competitors' products your potential customers have heard of, which they've bought and which they haven't. Just keep asking why – why did you buy it? Why did you stop buying it? Would you recommend it to a friend?

For most of your questions, they just won't remember or won't really know 'why' they did the things they did. But the point here is to get some clues as to what clever things your competitors do that you can copy. Or what things they're doing a terrible job of that you can maybe do better.

When you're interviewing potential customers, make sure you set the tone right. You're really just having a conversation with another human being about your idea – let the conversation go wherever it goes, rather than sticking to a rigid script. If you can take the approach of simply asking for people's advice, they won't feel threatened by your call.

Once you've done half an hour's worth of interviews, you should have enough clues from potential customers as to what your product needs to do. You may well decide that there is value to be had in talking to even more potential customers. Don't stop doing this until you feel that you've learned what you need to know for you to move on.

THE COMPETITION

🕐 Day 1, 10.42am

All businesses have some sort of competitor, or at least another company that you can look to for clues about what your customers expect. Once you launch your business, it's important to be customer-focused rather than competitor-focused. Having said that, when you're first starting out, the best way to get an idea of what your customers expect from you is to look at what the competition is offering.

We can assume that any of the successful businesses in your chosen field will have spent years perfecting their offering; figuring out what the best price is, which sizes people want to buy and so on. Since they've already done all of that work, why would you start from scratch and figure it all out again?

In this vein, you should view your competition as your free research and development department. Don't be afraid of taking inspiration from what they've already done, to help accelerate the process of getting your own business started.

I have a look around at some of the other brands against which I'm going to find myself competing. I try to figure out quickly what they're doing well and what they're doing not so well. A quick way to get a clue as to which brands are the most successful is to check out the category on Amazon or, in my case, an online supermarket. You can usually sort all of the products 'by popularity'.

By finding out which products are most successful, I can gain clues as to what my business should offer. You can make a little table showing the main competitors, listed in order of what size you think they are. Identify what you think they're doing well and what they're doing badly.

Name	What they do well?	What they do badly?
Quaker Oats Golden Syrup (£2.45/324g)	Individual sachets	Added sugar and flavouring
Rude Health 5 grain, 5 seed (£3.05/500g)	Premium packaging	Boring 'super-healthy' flavour
Dorset Cereals Oat & Barley (£2.59/420g)	Premium packaging	Boring 'super-healthy' flavour

Most popular brands of flavoured porridge oats, Waitrose, 2016.

The point of doing this is to get a quick idea of what has helped your most successful competitors get to where they are and also perhaps what has held back your least successful competitors.

What I learn from this super-quick analysis is that the most successful flavoured oat brands are around the same package weight – 300–500g. Unflavoured oats are typically packed in 1kg boxes. By going for a smaller weight, these premium brands can keep their price for the product within a sensible level (£2.45–£3.05).

It's also clear that quality packaging is really important to support this kind of gram-for-gram price premium over the regular oats. Based on what is popular on the shelves, there is an opportunity to launch a healthy but tasty brand. Currently, this isn't what's on offer from the leading brands.

ASK AN EXPERT

It's now an ideal time to use one of your special lifelines. You're ready to run your idea past someone who hopefully knows what they're talking about. I'm a huge fan of the value of asking the right questions of someone who has 'been there and done it before'. In fact, a lot of what I've learned about business has come from just asking for help.

Throughout my career, I've been amazed at how willing successful entrepreneurs are to share what they've learned with those who are trying to climb up the ladder behind them.

My parents have always been hugely supportive of my entrepreneurial efforts, but in my early teens I began having questions that they just didn't know the answers to, such as 'How much margin does a supermarket expect to make?' or 'Which agency should I use to design my packaging and what sort of budget should I offer them?'

In search of answers to these questions, my parents asked the neighbours if anyone knew an entrepreneur. One of the neighbours said, 'I work for this guy called Kevin Dorren … I guess he's an entrepreneur.'

I was soon introduced to him and so began a long friendship. He had started a successful business selling food products to supermarkets and had some really relevant experience. When he heard about my door-to-door jam selling it apparently made him laugh, reminding him of himself doing something similar as a small boy.

After I'd told him, over coffee, all about my idea and my plans to sell SuperJam to the big supermarkets, he gave me invaluable advice about packaging design, supermarket promotions and dealing with factories.

I've found that everyone who has built a successful business did so with the help and advice of others. Perhaps that's why, more often than not, they are happy to give advice in turn to other people setting out on the same path.

What's helpful about finding a mentor for your business idea is that they will be completely impartial. Ask them to pick holes in it, to suggest what they would do in your shoes and, perhaps, to make connections to people they know would be useful to you.

FINDING THE RIGHT MENTOR

In my view, what's most important is that you find someone who has started a business as similar as possible to the one you are trying to start. That way, they will have been through all of the steps you are about to face and can tell you exactly how they did it – what the practical, time-saving lessons they learned were.

Of course, you can't try speaking to those who are direct competitors; just someone who has used the same business model as you but for a different market.

CLARITY.FM

Perhaps you know some people you can phone right away to run your idea past without having to look too far. I also recommend, though, that you check out the service Clarity.fm. At this stage in the process, it is a valuable tool to find clarity about whether you're onto a good idea or whether there are holes in your plan that you haven't seen.

This service enables you to contact, almost instantly, some exceptionally experienced entrepreneurs, authors and advisors and ask them whatever you need to. You'll be charged a small fee, usually just a couple of dollars per minute, and you'll be amazed at the valuable information you can extract from a 20-minute phone call. It's kinda like one of those sex chat lines, but for entrepreneurs!

ASKING THE RIGHT QUESTIONS

Whether you are paying for someone's time or convincing them to let you pick their brains as a favour, you'll want the time you spend with them to be productive. It helps if you know exactly what you want to find out from them before starting the conversation.

As with interviewing potential customers, you want the discussion to flow naturally, rather than being confined by a pre-written script. It's important that your mentor enjoys talking to you, otherwise they won't put much effort into the activity or be up for meeting you a second or third time.

Try to find out what they have done in the past that worked – what actions they took that were successful. You're looking for tested, proven ways of doing things that you can copy. Anybody can give you a handful of unproven ideas, but only those who have started a similar business to the one you're working on can tell you what actually works.

Ask your mentor general things like:

- What are the things you tried that didn't work? Why do you think they didn't work?
- What changes have you made to your product over time?
- What do you wish you had done from day one?

- If you had the chance to start over again, how would you do it?
- What was the most effective form of marketing?
- How much did you have to spend on marketing to get one customer?
- How much does your average customer spend with them?
- What has caused the most complaints or problems for customers?
- What are your gross margins?

You might also ask some very specific questions, related to your particular industry, such as:

- What do you see as the main trends affecting the industry?
- What is the conversion rate on your Google ads?
- Where do you go for news and information about the industry?
- What blogs should I read?
- Which companies do you think are doing a good job and which aren't?
- What is your business going to do next?

By sticking to questions about what actions they have actually taken, what successes and failures they have had and what plans they are putting into place themselves, you can see where they are 'putting their money where their mouth is'.

It's easy for them to tell you what they think you should do, but it's much more useful to find out what they've actually done in their own business. What we really want is to find out what has worked for them and to copy it for our own concepts.

BEEF UP YOUR IDEA

🕐 Day 1, 11.00am

Based on all of the research I've done into the market and my interviews with prospective customers, I have a much clearer idea of what my product needs to be. Throughout this process, I'd strongly encourage you to make changes to your idea as and when you get new feedback or information.

Change one thing

When you're developing your idea, there is a huge temptation to try to completely reinvent every aspect of the product so as to be completely different to your competitors: to sell it in a different size of packet, at a different price, with unusual flavours and to a business model unlike anything offered by the competition.

It might well be that making one of these changes could provide the basis for a successful company, but if you change everything you'll just confuse the customer. For my product, there is a reason why all of the successful brands are packed in 300–500g packets and are selling through major supermarkets. It's because this package size keeps the price point within reasonable bounds, and supermarkets are where people want to buy it from.

THE FOUR Ps

The easiest way to define your idea is to write down the classic 'four Ps'. It sounds like boring marketing textbook stuff, but it offers a valuable checklist to ensure you've thought through the key facets of your idea.

Product – what am I selling?

My plan is to sell a range of three super-premium porridge oat mixes. They'll be packed beautifully, with a great packaging design. I want the flavours to be healthy but also indulgent and fun – something more interesting than the 'holier than thou' oat mixes that are already on the shelves, but healthier than the ones that are full of sugar.

Promotion – how will I let my customers know I exist?

We can talk in more detail later in this book about the different ways you can promote your business, but it's worth having an idea in your mind about where to start. You may well need to order some promotional materials today or brief a designer to create them.

To promote my product, I will most likely hand out samples in the local stores, possibly at farmers' markets and other events. I'd also like to try advertising online to see if I can find customers directly, rather than relying completely on sales to retailers. I think there's a good story about my product, so I'll try sending some samples to journalists, in the hope that they might write about it.

Place – where will my customers find me?

I'll be selling my oat mixes through retailers, primarily – my dream is to get the product into a supermarket, but I'll start out by supplying some small stores in the local area. I'd also like to sell directly to consumers through my own website, so that people who can't find them in their local store can still get hold of a pack.

Price

At this stage, I believe in making a 'back of an envelope' financial model for your business idea. Anything more detailed is usually an elaborate waste of time. Many entrepreneurs create vast financial models showing line after line of how they predict their business will be performing three, five or even ten years from now. I've even done it myself.

The problem with creating these complex models is that they are based on extrapolating from unproven assumptions that are always at least a bit wrong. In reality, everything will be tougher and take longer than you predict. Your business will also evolve so much and so quickly that these models will become redundant within days of being created.

So why do people devise these complex financial models? Well, mostly because they're the best way of giving people like banks, investors and government agencies the false impression that you know what you're doing. Of course, you don't – nobody running a start-up really does. You're working on an idea, a bunch of assumptions and, to be honest, a lot of optimism.

So what financial planning is actually useful? Well, the way I look at it, everything boils down to a simple question of how much you need to charge for your product in order to make a profit. If that price is higher than what you think customers are willing to pay, then you need to tweak the product or the model until you get to a price that works.

This sounds simplistic but I really think that pricing is the question you need to answer, because if you get this right, everything else will follow.

The middle of the road is a dangerous place to be

When it comes to what price you should charge for your product, I have an overarching theory that I'd like to share with you. It may not be relevant for every business and market but it is a trend that every entrepreneur should think about when deciding on how to price their product.

In the past, the most successful companies in the world went after the middle ground, but this has now changed. The most successful companies today are not usually those who follow this strategy.

In the twentieth century, the companies that grew large and rich won this race for the middle – McDonald's, Kellogg's, Heinz. They created products that almost everyone buys, no matter if they are rich or poor. They are not the most expensive, nor are they the cheapest.

But now, in the twenty-first century, the middle has already been taken by these established companies – the middle market is so competitive that, to succeed, new brands must focus on the edges, by creating either discount brands that undercut the big brands, or luxury products that offer something more, mean something more or create a stronger emotional connection with their customers.

In fact, the companies in the middle are typically in decline, with the opportunity for growth now lying at the fringes. Many of the fastest-growing companies in the world over the past ten years have not been those offering products with a middle-of-the-road price. They are those whose prices are either super-cheap or super-expensive.

If you think of the wild success in the past ten years of Ryanair (or Southwest Airlines in the US), Primark, Poundland,

Aldi, Uber and Amazon, it is clear that by being the cheapest brand in the market you can really clean up. You can totally disrupt an existing market just through the strategy of being cheapest. Sure, all of these companies had more going for them than just their low prices, but they wouldn't have been such a success without them.

If you adopt the strategy of being the cheapest, as you grow you can invest the savings you make and lower your prices even more. It becomes a virtuous cycle that makes it hard for anyone else to come along and compete with you.

At the other end of the scale, if you think about companies like Apple, Nespresso, Aesop, Innocent Smoothies and Tesla, it's clear that you can also be a success by being the most expensive company in your category. All of these were bold enough to launch products that were wildly more expensive than those of their peers.

When you choose the route of being the most expensive, you are partly putting a flag in the ground that says 'we are the best'. But beyond that, you are able to earn margins that allow you to invest in marketing and product improvements that help you to cement your position as the best – which also makes it hard for someone else to come along and compete with you.

The gap between rich and poor is growing all around the world. Markets are polarising, and the middle class is being squeezed. An increasingly large number of people are on tighter budgets, while the number of wealthy consumers is also growing. This growing income inequality means that the market for discount brands is growing, as is the market for luxury goods, all at the same time.

Whichever path you choose, don't hesitate to show the boldness needed to be either the cheapest or the most expensive within your chosen market. At one of these extremes is the safest place to be, rather than right in the middle of the road with everyone else.

Setting my price

⏱ Day 1, 11.32am

As you can probably guess, for my premium oats business my plan will be to launch the most expensive brand in the category, not the cheapest. So the first step is to take a look at what is already on the supermarket shelves.

The most expensive brand on the shelves, gram for gram, is also the most popular: 'Nature's Path' sachets, in a multipack of different flavours. They're on sale at £1.12p per 100g. Since the quality of the product that I want to create will justify it being the most expensive brand in the category, I'll work on the idea that my oats should be, say, 10 per cent more expensive than theirs: £1.23 per 100g.

In my mind, £3 per pack seems like an ideal price point to aim for, based on the fact that the most successful brands are around that level. This means that I should work on creating packaging to hold around 250g of finished product.

That's the easy part. The big question is whether it is possible to make a profit from selling at that price. We now need to work back from the price on the shelf, taking into account all of the costs we expect to have, to figure out if it's even imaginable that we can make money at that price. If not, we will need to change something about the product or the business model to make it work.

Ultimately, my plan is to sell my product through stores, as well as through my own website, so here's a quick breakdown of how I think each of these channels will work.

Selling through stores

⏱ Day 1, 11.38am

The first thing to understand is what sort of margin a store would need to make on your product. For most items, you can expect this to be 30–50 per cent. It depends on lots of factors, but for the sake of this exercise let's assume a retailer will need to make 40 per cent on selling my product.

- Retail price ... £3
- Retailer margin (40%) ... £1.20
- **Price to retailer ... £1.80**

Thankfully there is no VAT (sales tax) on my product; if there were, I'd need to take it off here to know the net amount I'd be receiving for each item after I pay the government their cut (which, with the VAT rate at 20 per cent, would be 36p out of £1.80).

The costs of the product can be broken down into a few components that I can easily estimate the cost of. It doesn't take long to check the prices for buying these in bulk online. Rough numbers are fine.

- Oats ... 35p
- Dried fruit/nuts/chocolate ... 25p
- Cardboard tube packaging ... 45p
- Cost of labour to pack the tubes ... 15p
- Plastic lid ... 5p
- Label printing ... 5p
- **Total cost ... £1.30**

Based on these very rough costs, from selling through stores it looks like I can expect to make a margin of around 50p per unit, or about 30 per cent on the price at which I'm selling to the retailers. This isn't an incredible margin, but assuming I can make some cost savings over time it will probably work out about right.

Every business and product is different, but for a business selling a food product through retailers you want to aim for at least a 40 per cent gross margin. It may start out less in the early days, such as the 30 per cent I have calculated previously. Hopefully, as volumes grow, there will be cost savings that help to increase it to this level. This healthy margin structure will give you the ability to run price promotions and invest in advertising to grow your sales.

Selling through my own site

⏱ Day 1, 11.50am

As well as finding retailers to sell my oats, I would like to sell direct to consumers through my own website. The web can be the greatest channel of all – not only do you not have to convince a retailer to sell your product, you also have direct contact with your customers so you can learn about what they think of it. You also don't have to share your margin with anyone!

Selling through a website, I decide that the retail price should be the same as it is in the stores: £3. Although I don't have to share this sales revenue with a retailer, I do have to pay a credit card processor such as Stripe, PayPal or GoCardless a small fee (1–4 per cent, depending on sales volume) and will also have to cover the cost of postage.

Normally, an online store will have a free-delivery policy if customers spend over a certain amount. My gut feeling is that customers will only want to buy small amounts, let's say three packs, and that they will be put off by any high delivery costs. A fair price for P&P, I decide, would be £2; free for orders over £25. Let's see how that works:

Based on customer buying three packs

- Retail price (£3 per pack x 3 packs typical order) ... £9
- Delivery charge ... £2
- **Total revenue ... £11**

- Cost of products (3 x £1.30) ... ⁻£3.90
- Cost of postage ... ⁻£3.00*
- Payment processing charge (4%) ... ⁻£0.44
- Cost to me of cardboard postage box ... ⁻£0.30
- **Total costs ... ⁻£7.64**

- **Total margin ... £3.36 (30%)**

As you can see, although I don't have to share sales with a retailer, by the time I pay for the cost of postage, the margin works out about the same.

These 'back of a fag packet' calculations have given me enough confidence that, if I price my oats at £3, I'll be able to make money. The only thing I need to consider now is what fixed costs I might have – that is to say, what things will I need to pay for just to be able to run my business?

Fixed costs

⏱ Day 1, 12:30pm

It's worth doing a quick sense-check of whether or not you think it will be possible to sell enough of your products to cover your fixed costs. You need, in other words, to estimate your total running costs for, say, a year and then calculate how many prod-

---

* You can easily get quotes for postage costs by checking rates at Royal Mail for small weight items, or by looking up a courier consolidator online and googling 'cheap parcels' if your package is a bit heavier.

ucts you would need to sell to generate enough gross profit to cover all of your costs. If that number seems impossibly high, then you need to rethink some aspect of either your product or your business model.

This is where every business really is different. For some ideas, you will need to consider the cost of renting a shop, a food truck or some other big overhead. In the case of my oats business, the fixed costs will be quite limited. I will have to invest in:

- Hiring a designer to create my brand and labels ... £500
- Getting the product developed and photographed ... £500
- Buying a template for my website ... £150
- Buying promotional materials ... £150
- **Total ... £1,300**

This leaves £200 to buy the ingredients and packaging to produce my first batch of oat mixes. If I invest £1,300 in starting my business, then with a £1.30 margin on each one I sell at full price to a retailer I will need to sell 1,000 units (£1,300/£1.30) to break even; after that point, I'm into profit.

This doesn't seem like a crazy figure, so I'm happy to continue on the assumption that by selling my product through some stores and my own site I'll be able to sell them in the thousands.

CHAPTER 4

THE PRODUCT

Whether you're selling an actual product, as I am, or offering more of a service, exactly how you want it to work is entirely down to you. This part of the process will depend so much on your idea that it is difficult for me to give you a step-by-step guide. However, there are a few tips and tricks I can provide you with concerning some of the different ways you might go about creating your product.

DO IT YOURSELF

There is a lot to be said for getting to the end of the day and feeling the satisfying sensation of having actually made something. In a world of computer screens and digital downloads, we have become hugely disconnected from the art of physically creating things.

Every week, I meet people who have quit their jobs in the city in pursuit of such a feeling. They've started baking, crafting, brewing, carving and painting – using their eyes and hands to make a beautiful product. Many reading this book will have dreams of doing something similar – of turning their craft into a career.

Despite the fact that you love your homemade products and everyone tells you they are wonderful, there is a long way to go before you have a commercially viable product in your hands. You will have to be sure you can make your product at home sufficiently quickly and cheaply to be able to offer it at a competitive price.

It's important when you price your homemade products that you place at least some value on your own time, otherwise you're not really running a business. If you are producing food or drink, you will have to get a food hygiene certificate (you can do a multiple-choice test online and get an instant certificate for very little money) and have your kitchen inspected by the local government authority.

For most products, there will be packaging requirements (for example, 'best before' dates, washing instructions, country of origin) that you must adhere to by law. You can probably do this simply by checking what information your competitors' products have on them, as they should be operating within the law. It is also worth checking this information with your local government authority (the Trading Standards Department of your local council, if you're in the UK).

ETSY.COM

One of the driving forces in the revolution of people leaving their desks and instead taking up sewing, knitting, jewellery making and other crafts has been Etsy. Roughly approximating to a giant eBay for handmade goods, Etsy allows anyone who is making products themselves to set up a shop front instantly, so that their products are available to customers all around the world.

I know of many people who derive all or most of their income from selling goods on Etsy, but the majority of people selling there are doing so just as a sideline. If you are making a product yourself, I'd definitely recommend having an Etsy store as part of your overall business plan.

PROTOTYPING

For almost any product, the first step will be to get to the point of having a fully functional prototype version that you can show to potential customers. In the case of a food product, this will be a small batch of items that you have probably made yourself by hand which you can use as samples to get some bigger orders before pressing the green light on outsourced manufacturing.

MAKER SPACES

A great opportunity to create a prototype of your product, whether it is a chair or a piece of jewellery, comes in the form of Maker Spaces. In a lot of cities around the world, there are workshops available to hire by the hour – inside them is all of the equipment you could possibly need to fashion your product.

3D PRINTING

One of the most exciting and hyped areas of technological advance at the moment is 3D printing. The cost of the equipment and necessary chemicals is falling all the time, making this technology increasingly accessible. Ultimately, many products will probably be 3D printed, but at the moment one of the most commercially viable uses of this technology is to create prototypes.

A quick Google search will reveal heaps of companies offering you a chance to send over your design files to be 3D printed on their equipment for a relatively small fee.

T-SHIRTS, MUGS, STICKERS, ETC.

If you're good at designing graphics, have something funny to say or are creating a brand around a particular niche theme, there are a number of terrific manufacture-on-demand services for general merchandise. Things like T-shirts, mugs, stickers, caps, bags, greetings cards, posters and iPhone cases can all be easily printed on a one-by-one basis.

Companies such as Zazzle, CafePress, Everpress, Merchify and Spreadshirt allow you to set up your own online store on their platform, upload your images and instantly offer your designs for sale printed on all kinds of products. Depending on the prices you set for your items, you can make a reasonable margin, and the great thing is that you don't have to find your own suppliers, hold any stock or even handle the orders.

This model allows you to focus on creating your brand, producing good designs and driving people to your site. Once they're there, you don't need to worry about the rest. Even huge companies like Disney use Zazzle for some of their merchandising, which shows that it is a model that works.

OUTSOURCED MANUFACTURING

'Outsourcing' can often be seen as a dirty word – synonymous with redundancies in the West and sweatshops in the East. It conjures up an image of vast call centres in Mumbai staffed by thousands of enthusiastic young Indian operatives, frantically cold-calling English housewives in the middle of *Coronation Street*, to try their luck at selling them a new mobile phone contract.

Contract manufacturing, as it is otherwise known, is often thought of as the antithesis of the 'maker' revolution. However, in my experience, it doesn't have to be that way. In fact, most outsourcing doesn't even involve sending work overseas – it is simply about finding someone with production facilities who can make your product for you.

Outsourcing is all about finding companies that can do a better, cheaper and more efficient job of tasks than you can on your own. The key is figuring out what the core of your business is – designing products, for example – and then finding companies who are better than you at everything else. By involving other companies in your idea, it is possible to scale up production incredibly quickly, without the risk of investing in your own plant and machinery.

In fact, a huge proportion of the brands that we buy every day use outsourced manufacturing. This is because they have decided they should focus their energy on building brands, marketing and developing new products, and let someone else take care of the messy job of production, warehousing and distribution.

I built SuperJam on the back of being able to find a 120-year-old jam company who believed in my idea. At 17 years old, I obviously wasn't in a position to build my own jam factory, and so I had to convince an existing factory to work with me to make my products on a big scale.

After travelling around the country, from the tiny islands in Scotland to the big cities in England, I came across one company that had some spare capacity and felt that my idea to make jam 100 per cent from fruit was worth a shot. Some months later, we figured out how to produce my recipes on a large scale and were able to supply supermarkets.

When you are looking for someone to manufacture your product for you, there are a number of things to consider. This will be the most important relationship in your whole business, so it is important that you find the right company to work with. If your partner turns out to be prone to mistakes, late deliveries and poor quality, all of these things will negatively affect your brand and could cost you in terms of customer loyalty.

Ideally, you want to visit the factory yourself to fully understand how your products will be made, how the cost is made up and what you can do to speed up the process of getting your idea into production.

However, given we are hoping to get your business off the ground in the next couple of days, the most important thing will be to find a factory that can agree in principle to produce a first batch of product for you. You will need them to create a master sample, or a prototype, that you can use for photography to display on your site.

The biggest stumbling block you will face with any manufacturer is agreeing upon minimum order quantities. From the factory's point of view, your idea is a headache – factory managers hate new ideas. If they could, they would make the same product all day, every day, without the need to change parts in between production runs.

You will want as small an initial production run as possible, to limit your risk in case nobody ends up buying your product. And, of course, the factory will want you to commit to as large a run as possible. You can always get them to agree to a smaller first order by paying upfront and promising that your subsequent orders will be larger.

PRIVATE LABEL

The simplest and fastest way to get your idea onto the production line is simply to 'private label' a manufacturer's existing product. This is where you literally buy a product that the factory makes anyway, but give it your own packaging.

If you are selling something that is fairly commoditised, such as vitamin supplements or razor blades, it should be very easy to find a factory that is happy to produce these for you under your own brand. In fact, chances are, most of their existing business is based on supplying supermarket own-label products.

A key thing to bear in mind is that because of the nature of private-label manufacturing, your product will not be particularly unique or special – there will already be other people in the market selling the exact same items, just under a different name. So it's vital that the way you are delivering or branding it is radically different if you want to have any chance of attracting customers.

CHINESE MANUFACTURING

The problems associated with outsourcing production can easily be multiplied by adding the extra layer of complexity that working with a factory overseas brings. That said, despite the occasional language barrier, factories in China and elsewhere are generally very keen to service your requirements and can usually get samples shipped to you next day.

All of SuperJam's products are manufactured in the UK and, for food products at least, domestic production is probably the best option. We would probably all love to live in a world where everything was locally produced, but unfortunately we don't and embracing overseas manufacturing can present some great opportunities for entrepreneurs.

What is top of most people's minds when we talk about Chinese manufacturing is ethical considerations, especially the working conditions of the people who are involved. Being so far away, it is unlikely to be practical for you to visit the factories you are speaking to in person. You can, however, check their ratings via third-party agencies that conduct inspections. These vary between different types of factory but you will be able to ask your factory for more details about their levels of certification.

ALIBABA

The internet has made the world a much smaller place, from the point of view of finding manufacturing partners in faraway countries. In the past, you would have had to deal with brokers, agents, importers, exporters, distributors, translators, chambers of commerce and all kinds of other intermediaries. Now, you can very easily contact the factory directly and begin a dialogue right away.

The biggest and easiest site to use to contact potential manufacturing partners is Alibaba.com. It is predominantly focused on Chinese factories but there are also companies from all over the world. You'll find listings for every conceivable kind of product – from toothpicks to tablet computers and everything in between.

You can simply search for companies that make the products you are looking for, and then send your specifications to those you think look up to the job. They'll get back to you, usually in a matter of hours, with their estimated costs, sample costs, timescales and delivery and payment terms.

Once you have got your shortlist down to your favourite, you will probably want to send them a sample of your product, which they can then simply copy. For some products this won't be an option, in which case just make sure that your specifications are extremely detailed.

SELF-PUBLISHING

If your product is a book, you should consider publishing it yourself using one of a number of services that allow you to upload your content, edit it online and then offer it for sale on a print-on-demand basis. This way, so long as you have created the content, you can have your book available for sale almost immediately.

I like to say that all businesses have a book in them; if you are selling food, make a cookbook. If you're selling holidays, make a coffee-table photo book about some of the destinations you have on offer. And if you're running a guesthouse or tour guide business, you could create a guidebook about your city.

People really trust books; they assume that the author has something interesting to say and that the book they've written has gone through some kind of editing process. People also rarely throw books away – which makes them an incredibly powerful marketing tool.

BLURB

My favourite self-publishing site, Blurb.com, makes it really easy to create incredibly beautiful, high-print-quality books. It is perfect for something like a cookbook, photo book, guidebook or children's book, since the production values are extremely high.

However, with this high quality comes a price – the cover price of books that you make with Blurb will end up being particularly high, which makes them really just suited for small projects and for books that showcase what you do, rather than being your main product in and of themselves.

AMAZON CREATESPACE

A very viable way to publish your work is directly with Amazon, which is of course where the vast majority of books are sold these days. Their system makes it easy for you to offer your work as a print-on-demand book or eBook and they simply pay you a royalty on the sale of each copy sold, which will typically work out at a lot more per copy than you would receive from a tradi-tional publisher.

DROP SHIPPING

You may not even need to create your own products at all, but could rather become a retailer for other people. To avoid having to carry stock, it is possible to create a catalogue of products online for your customer to order, and then send these orders straight to the manufacturer to dispatch. You can negotiate a discounted price to pay the manufacturer, giving you a margin for effectively being the middleman. This process is called drop shipping, and can be very effective so long as you find the right products to sell.

For example, you could create a site that promotes food and drink produced in your local area. You could build a site, populate it with products that are on sale at your local farmers' market and then send the order straight to the small producers to dispatch to customers. Perhaps they don't sell their products online but would be happy to receive some extra business.

APPS

We've long since crossed the point where there is more web traffic on mobile phones than on desktop computers, so the opportunity to set up your business 'mobile first' can certainly be appealing. Lots of businesses have had huge success by going down this route – Deliveroo, Uber, YPlan and HotelTonight are just a few brilliant examples.

The first question you need to answer is whether or not your idea actually needs to be an app – would a mobile-optimised website be more appealing to your customers than an actual app?

If you're sure that your model requires customers to download (for free or paid) an actual app, then just like building a website you have a couple of options for how to do it. Either you can use one of a number of 'drag and drop' tools to help you quickly and cheaply build it yourself, or you can hire a developer to build something bespoke for you.

MAGAZINES

There is something beautiful about a printed magazine – a piece of work that someone has taken the time to put together on a particular niche topic. With our magazine, *Ferment*, we have learned a lot about how to publish a high-quality publication on a limited budget.

The magazine business is extremely difficult to make any money from, but if you can build enough of a following for your publication, of course you can find ways of making money from selling subscriptions, advertising, sponsorship, live events and commercial partnerships.

The first step in creating a successful publication is finding great content – you will have your own particular sphere of interest that you want to write about and it will be down to you to find contributors, photographers and other people who believe in your vision enough to support it with free or cheap content to help get it off the ground in the early days. Even though you're producing your content on a low budget for a limited audience in the beginning, what's important is that you create something absolutely of the best standard you can – something that people will actually want to subscribe to, tell their friends about or buy advertising in.

To help finance your first print run, you could sell annual subscriptions to people who believe in your concept sufficiently that they are willing to part with a decent amount of money to see it happen. You'd be amazed at the number of people who would value being a 'founding member' of a new publication and you should do what you can to make them feel special and involved in your exciting new journey.

The goal for your 48-hour start-up project should be to create a site that gives people a taster of what your magazine will be about. You can then use that as a platform to sell subscriptions or pre-orders to your network.

There are a number of print-on-demand services (such as Blurb) that will help you to create a magazine without having to invest heavily in the production of thousands of copies before you know if they're going to sell. These services also make it very easy to design, edit and lay out your magazine with their own proprietary software. When someone places an order, the service provider prints a copy of your magazine; simple as that.

In our experience with *Ferment*, the biggest thing we have learned is how important photography is in the creation of a great magazine. So, either make sure you can shoot fantastic images yourself or get someone on board who can.

If you want to sell your magazine through stores, you'll need to register an ISSN number with the British Library or with the equivalent in your own country. If you produce your publication in a standard size, such as A4, this will help to keep print costs under control.

The chances are that the main way you will monetise your publication will be through selling advertising. Selling ad space in a new magazine can be challenging, so a brilliant technique is to give the space away for free to brands that you'd love to carry. Then you can go to other brands and say, 'Hey, look at all these great brands that advertise with us.' This can really help to position your magazine in a way that gives the right impression to potential paid advertisers and bring in some ad sales quickly.

Whether you are producing a magazine, a brochure or some other type of printed material, I can recommend using Adobe InDesign. You should be able to get a free month's trial to play around with it. A useful trick also is to download free or paid templates – these are pre-designed magazine or brochure layouts that you can very easily use to drop your own images and text into. You can become a publisher of your own magazine, bringing your passion for your topic to life, without any particular design skills.

YOUTUBE

There are a lot of people out there who make money from their content through uploading it to YouTube. By carrying pre-roll ads and link ads in your video, you'll be able to make a small amount of money every time someone watches it. This could be a possible way of monetising your passion for baking, for example, by creating a free online set of tutorials for people to watch.

CREATING THE AWESOME OATS PRODUCT

⏱ Day 1, 12.45pm

Already I have a pretty clear idea of what I want my product to be like, but since I am not a chef I decide that my concept would benefit from a professional's experience. I set out to find a 'food designer'; someone who can take my basic idea and turn it into a finished, delicious product.

Porridge isn't necessarily the sexiest product in the world, so to create a premium brand I'm going to need a chef who can help me to create some appealing images of what I'm selling.

I manage to find someone who is perfect for the job – a food stylist in London called Alexandre Paganelli, who runs a studio called DeadHungry.co. Not only is he a great chef – he's also a talented photographer who can help me to create my products and then shoot them to create images for our website. His style is very minimal and he makes the food he shoots look really delicious; his talent will be put to good work in making porridge look sexy and fun.

When I tell Alex about the concept for my premium oat mixes, he agrees to help me out with developing the recipes today and shooting the finished product tomorrow. It's a fast turnaround for a product like this but he's up for the challenge.

With the help of my '48-hour food stylist', I come up with a range of flavours for my mixes. It's important that they are delicious but also natural and vegan, so that we can promote them as a healthy indulgence. I want the range to offer flavours that are sufficiently mainstream for me not to alienate potential customers, but that also offer a wide enough range to appeal to a number of different tastes.

Day 1, 1:05pm

Flavours:

- Dark chocolate, orange peel and hazelnuts.
- Peanut, banana and chia seed.
- Apple, raisins, cinnamon and pecans.

I know from talking to my local store and looking at my successful competitors that creating premium packaging designs is going to be critical to the success of my brand. I've also been advised by my local store not to pack my product into bags, but rather to use something more substantial.

Looking at packaging for 'oatmeal' in America on the packaging blog TheDieline, I notice that a lot of brands are packed into attractive, round, cardboard canisters with metal lids. I figure that this sort of packaging could be perfect for my product and will really help me to stand out on the shelf, given that most of the brands I'll be competing against are packed in boring rectangular boxes.

⏱ Day 1, 1:15pm

After some quick googling, I manage to track down a UK company called Visican, which specialises in this type of packaging. I send them an email, explaining that I am working on an urgent product development project. By explaining that my ultimate goal for the project is to supply supermarkets, I figure that they should be excited enough by the idea to help me out with some samples so that I can make an initial small batch of products.

Soon after I get in touch, they reply to say that it would be no problem for them to send me a box of cardboard tubes that they have in stock. They also provide me with a quote so that I know how much the tubes will cost once I go into production.

A set of cardboard tubes is on its way for next-day delivery, Alex has completed testing out some recipes and it looks like everything is on track to have a finished product ready to sell by tomorrow.

SANDOW'S COLD BREW COFFEE

How to start a food and drink brand from home

I caught up with the founders of London's increasingly successful cold brew coffee company, Sandow's. Hugh Duffie and Luke Suddards set up the company in Hackney Wick after they saw the cold brew coffee trend take off in the US and they have now seen their products launch in stores across the city, including in the likes of Selfridges and Marks & Spencer.

They started out on a tiny scale, developing their cold brew recipes in their flat. They'd brew up batches and test them out on friends and family. Once they had a recipe that was popular, they brewed up 100 bottles, packaged them beautifully and gave them to people they respected in the industry, asking for their feedback.

They agreed that if the response was positive they'd go into it full time. Overwhelmed by the positivity that greeted their product and its packaging, they decided to pursue their idea further.

They have some excellent advice for anyone trying to create a professional-looking brand from home:

> You need to make sure that your packaging is within the law; that you include your address and the weight; all of that stuff will become obvious over time with a bit of research. But what's perhaps more important is what you want people to see when they look at your brand. We went through multiple different designs and even brand names until we got to the brand that we settled on.

You can listen to the full interview on the *48-Hour Start-Up* podcast show at 48hourstartup.org.

CHAPTER 5

CREATING A KICK-ASS BRAND

Earlier in the book I spoke about the idea that 'USP is dead', by which I meant that it is unlikely that your product will be truly unique. What you do have that is unique, however, is your story, your ethos and eventually the culture of your team.

If I reflect on my own experience of growing SuperJam, I'd say that all I really own is a brand. We don't have our own factory and our recipes are so natural and simple that anyone could make them themselves, so there are no trade secrets or patents to speak about.

When you set up a business in the way that I am advocating in this book, it's most likely that all you'll really end up owning is a brand. You may well outsource many of the functions of your business to other companies and to freelancers, rather than setting up your own manufacturing or building a team. Because of this it's super-important that every decision you make and everything you do is helping to build your brand.

It's of critical importance that your product, website, marketing and everything else looks amazing. This is especially true if you're running a predominantly online business; the only way that people can tell the quality of what you're offering is with their eyes – they can't taste it, smell it or really talk to you about it.

In the case of a food business, the aesthetics are unbelievably crucial to the overall success of the venture. In the case of SuperJam, I learned early on that no matter how good the jam in the jar was, if it didn't look great, nobody would take it off the shelves to find out.

In preparation for my second pitch to Waitrose, I worked with an advertising agency to create the SuperJam brand. We figured that there was a link between SuperJam and Superman, or so we thought, and decided to create the packaging around a comic book theme. We covered the labels and lids with jokes and puns. I thought that if I could make people laugh enough, then maybe they'd buy my product! I would be Jam Boy, a superhero character, with a costume and everything!

Of course, when it came time to present this idea to the supermarket buyers, they didn't see the funny side. They explained that packaging wasn't there to make people laugh – it was there to get a message across; to answer the fundamental question of why anybody should buy my product.

Even though I, and all of my teenaged friends, thought that the comic book idea was hilarious, I decided to listen to the supermarket buyers, throw the designs in the bin and start all over again.

When I was having this hard time with the packaging designs, I wrote to a number of companies that I thought had done a great job of designing their packaging, to ask for their advice. Even though their products were completely different to my own, there was inspiration I could take from what they'd done and lessons I could learn from their success.

One brand that I learned from was called Method. They make cleaning products in the US and, I have to say, this was the first time in my life that I had any interest in cleaning products. But what I realised was that they had innovated with products such as toilet cleaner – products that usually are so ugly and badly designed that people hide them away underneath the kitchen sink and don't even think about them. They had gone against the grain and created something that was, in its own way, beautiful – something that people wouldn't be afraid to leave lying around their home for guests to see.

Method's success showed me that, no matter what your product is, with good design and a fresh attitude it can look beautiful.

Another brand that I got a lot of inspiration from, funnily enough given my new adventures in oats, was Dorset Cereals, a UK granola and muesli company. Their packaging is extremely simple – only using one or two colours and saying just what needs to be said. In fact, by being so simple, their brand is actually able to stand out in comparison to the really noisy, colourful brands like Kellogg's Coco-Pops, sitting beside them on the shelves.

But definitely the brand that I got the most design inspiration from was Innocent. They're a UK smoothie and fruit juice company who have completely redefined how everyone in this country thinks about packaging. On the back of their bottles and cartons their tone of voice talks to consumers as if they are just chatting to a friend in the pub. This style has been copied so widely that it doesn't always wear well on every brand, but at the time it was pioneering.

HAVE ONE MESSAGE

I was able to meet with Dan Germain, the man who created the Innocent brand. He told me all kinds of things about packaging but one thing he said really stuck in my mind. Too many people, he told me, try to say, 'Here are ten reasons for why you should buy my product.' He figured that the key to success in branding was just picking one good reason and putting all of your time and energy into trying to get that one message across. If you make it really simple then, maybe, when someone is spending half a second looking at your product on the supermarket shelves they will get your message. And maybe, if they get your message, they may buy your product.

Having taken on board Dan's advice, I realised that SuperJam just had to focus on getting its message of 100 per cent fruit across. And since then, our packaging hasn't changed and has definitely been a key part of the company's success.

So I would say that before you rush into putting pen to paper and designing your branding, you should absolutely crystallise in your own mind why someone should buy your product.

🕐 Day 1, 1:32pm

An excellent way to think about this is to imagine what some-one would say to their partner should they be asked why they've spent their hard-earned money on something. They might say, 'Because it's great value for money' or 'Because it's ethical' or 'Because it'll help me to learn something new.'

For my oat-mix idea, I think someone would justify their purchase to their partner by saying the reason they picked it up at the shop was 'Because it comes in fun flavours.'

Now that you have such a simple summary of what you're creating, it'll be really easy to come up with a name, strapline and overall look and feel for your brand. Without such a clear one-line summary of why someone should buy your product, you'll be stabbing in the dark.

PICKING A NAME

🕐 Day 1, 1.36pm

In my view, a lot of people fret over what to call their business; they spend weeks and even months trying to come up with the perfect name. The truth is, your name will always only be a word or a couple of words that don't really mean anything. That is, they won't mean anything until your customers decide what that name means to them, based on the product you deliver and the experience that you give them. That's the point at which a mere word becomes a brand.

So, having reflected on my own experience of spending many weeks racking my brain trying to come up with names for other ideas in the past, I believe you can do this much more quickly, with a little bit of help.

My suggestion is just to pick a name that is catchy enough that people won't immediately forget it and, most importantly, that you can get a domain name for, without infringing anyone's trademark.

There are a number of brilliant tools to help you come up with a domain name in seconds: BustAName.com allows you to input all of the words related to your idea; it sticks them together and shows you which combinations are available as domain names for you to register.

NameStation.com lets you run a competition, where real people brainstorm domain name ideas for you and you are able to select the one that you like the best; the person who suggested the one you choose wins a prize.

⏱ Day 1, 1:36pm

I decide to use BustAName for my oats business, since it offers an instant solution and I am, after all, working to a tight deadline. I put in all of the words that I can think of to do with my idea: oats, porridge, breakfast, healthy, great, delicious, fun, amazing, awesome, tasty, flavours, Scottish, exciting.

If you need help doing this, you can very quickly put your ideas into an online thesaurus, which will instantly give you more options.

I flick through the list of suggestions and immediately spot AwesomeOats.com, which I think sounds pretty cute and fits nicely with my theme of making fun flavours of 'pimped-up porridge oats'. My childish sense of humour also thinks there's something funny about my first product being Super and my second being Awesome … or maybe I'm just not that good at coming up with names after all.

Registering a domain name is super-easy; you just need to visit one of the major domain registering sites. GoDaddy.com is the biggest but there are hundreds of others and they very often have special offers, so shop around.

🕐 Day 1, 1.48pm

WHAT IF YOUR DREAM NAME IS ALREADY REGISTERED?

Just like the actual name of your business, I don't think the domain name is as important as people imagine, especially if most of your sales will come from offline sources. So don't waste time trying to find the perfect domain. If, however, you have your heart set on buying a domain that someone else already owns, there's a couple of ways you can go about it.

Many domains are listed on 'aftersales markets', such as Sedo. com, so you can check them out there. But usually the best approach is to contact domain owners directly – which is pretty easy to do by searching for the domain name on the who.is website. You can try negotiating hard via email – they will always start out with a ludicrous figure and, depending on the name, you should be able to beat them down to a few hundred pounds.

I once managed to buy the domain name Haggis.com (Scotland's national dish) in exactly this way, for only a few hundred pounds. I did have an idea to sell haggis online, especially around Burns Night and in America, but later found out that it has been banned in the USA since the 1970s, because it contains sheep's lung. Having since become a vegetarian, I have no plans to go into the haggis business now, but it did teach me the lesson that you can get your hands on great domain names more inexpensively than you might imagine.

TRADEMARKS

Some TV entrepreneurship shows would give you the impression that it's hugely important to protect your intellectual property, to file a patent and register a trademark. Chances are, however, that what you're doing isn't so ground-breaking that it warrants a patent, and registering a trademark is only really important when you're absolutely sure that your idea is what the market wants and you plan to scale it up.

At this stage, I wouldn't worry too much about protecting your IP. Of course, if your business takes off then you'll want to apply for a trademark, which costs a couple of hundred quid. But, for now, I think it is an unnecessary distraction. What is important, however, is that you check you will not be infringing on someone else's trademark.

In the UK, you can check on the Intellectual Property Office's website – www.ipo.gov.uk. Just do a quick search for the name that you have chosen to be sure that nobody else has already laid claim to the name or phrase you are hoping to use, within the product category you will be selling in.

For companies in the US, you'll want to do a search via the United States Patent and Trademark Office at www.uspto.gov. Every other country has their own equivalent and, if you are planning to launch your business in foreign markets one day, it will be worthwhile checking all of the relevant databases before you do.

Day 1, 1.59pm

I run a very quick check of 'awesome' in the relevant product categories for selling porridge oats and, thankfully, there's nobody using that name for anything. I'm all clear to register my domain name and start building a brand.

WRITING A STRAPLINE

Not all businesses have a 'strapline', otherwise known as a slogan, and it's not totally necessary, but you may well want to add one to your brand. If you don't decide to do it now, it's something that you can always add at a later date, to save yourself time for the present. It's basically just a sentence which conveys the whole point of your business' existence in a second. What do you sell and why should someone buy it?

It's a little tricky to change the name of your business after you launch, since people will start to get attached to it from day one. Your strapline, on the other hand, can easily be changed over time if you come up with something better or alter the message that you want to give your customers about your product.

Day 1, 2.03pm

You have already established what your product is ('a range of premium, tasty, pre-mixed porridge oats') and why someone should buy it ('tastes more exciting than the other brands'). All you have to do now is find a fun, catchy way of getting this message across that fits well with the name you have chosen.

In my case, I've already been describing my project as 'pimped-up porridge oats', which I kinda like. Sometimes the best ideas are the first ones that come into your head, so I'm happy just to run with this one.

But supposing I didn't already have an idea for a strapline; one quick approach would be simply to write down all the words related to your product, just like you have done to create a name, but perhaps expanding on the themes of this key message you want to communicate.

Then try combining some of your favourite words, along with your brand name, to create something appealing. This will take a few attempts, but don't be afraid of throwing lots of things at the wall and seeing what sticks. Since this is something that we can change at a later date, you should only aim to come up with something that is 'good enough' and just run with it.

CREATING A MOOD BOARD

⏱ Day 1, 2:10pm

The most rapid way to kick-start the design process for your new brand is to create a simple 'mood board'. This is where you collect a few images together that will give the designer a good sense of the look and feel you are aiming for. It's good to consider what other brands your target consumer may like to buy, what image it is that you are trying to convey and what brands you think are doing a good job of getting similar messages across.

I would say that the best sites to look at for inspiration are Behance, TheDieline, Lovely Package, Designspiration and Dribbble. These are all sites that feature designers' portfolios from around the world. You can easily search by theme ('oats' for example), substrate (such as cardboard) or category (focusing on photography, logos, etc.).

To speed up the design process, it will be helpful if you can find some fonts that you like, which your designer can use. If you don't feel comfortable doing this, don't worry, your designer will of course be able to do this for you. Some good sites to look at for beautiful free fonts are Fontfabric.com, LostType.com and MyFonts.com. If you have the budget for it, you can of course find paid fonts that are even more beautiful. YouWorkForThem is probably my favourite site from which to buy fonts.

Whatever elements your brand needs to contain, try to create a mood board that captures a sense of what the font should feel like, what style the videos and photography should be, and what mood your colour palette should convey.

There are lots of online pin boards that you can use to collect all of your different inspirations in one place, so that you can easily send your designer a link to view your mood board. You can use Pinterest, or I personally like Springpad.com, where you can clip elements from all over the internet or upload images directly from your computer.

The point here is to translate your brand's 'one message' (i.e. that we are making porridge fun) into images. This 'mood board' can be used to help brief a designer or, if you're planning to do the design yourself, can help to focus the mind on what style you need to create.

Designers are visual people, so communicating with images will help to avoid the misunderstanding that can happen if you try explaining your vision with words. And, since we don't have much time, we need to make sure that the designer strikes a hole in one.

You can see my Pinterest mood board at 48hourstartup.org.

Day 1, 2.22pm

HIRING A DESIGNER VS 'DIY'

If you're lucky enough to have some design skills of your own, it may be the case that you can create at least the initial version of your brand for no money, by yourself. The only caution that I would give is that I come across many people who 'had a go' at designing their brand themselves, and ended up creating something that doesn't do their idea justice.

Quite often, I meet entrepreneurs who show me something they have designed by themselves and ask me what I think. More often than not it is terrible, and I have a hard time telling them that their baby is ugly. Be careful that when you show your designs to family and friends they aren't just telling you what you want to hear, to avoid hurting your feelings. Try to show the work to people who can be objective about it and consider not telling them that you designed it yourself, so that they're even more likely to be honest with you.

On these grounds, it is likely that almost every business will require the work of a designer to create a logo and a brand image that will be good enough to entice people to want to buy from you. No matter how good your product is, if the website doesn't look good or your packaging isn't attractive, nobody is going to buy from you to find out.

This is definitely a part of the whole process that a lot of people are terrified by. They worry that designers are incredibly expensive and that they need to have some kind of special ability to know how to direct them in creating their brand.

My advice, first of all, is to be very clear about what the message is that your brand is trying to communicate. In my case, I want to create one that says 'fun porridge oats'. If your message is as clear as that, anybody stopping by your site, or picking up your packaging in the store, even if just for a few seconds, will get it.

You would be amazed at how quickly you can find yourself a brilliant designer. There are all kinds of sites that offer you designers who are willing to work on your project from home, by the hour and for extremely competitive prices.

My personal favourite approach is to make a mood board for what I'm trying to create and then just track down and contact the particular designers who worked on the brands I'm inspired by. They can usually be contacted directly through their own websites or you can find their work through one of the portfolio sites I mentioned before. That way, you know they can deliver something of the style and standard you're after.

Once you pick a designer to work with, trust them. They are professionals at what they do and will have a good idea of what works and what doesn't. Having said that, don't be afraid of telling them if the logo they come back with isn't up to scratch or if you'd like them to make small changes; that is all included in the original price you agreed to pay.

Don't be afraid of breaking the project down into steps, with different amounts payable at each stage. For example, you might get the designer to work on your logo first and then, assuming you're happy with the output, move on to the next stages later. It's also typical to pay 50 per cent upfront and then 50 per cent on completion. Both of these methods mean that you don't have to take all the risk if their designs end up not being as great as you'd hoped.

FREELANCER MARKETPLACES

Aside from contacting designers directly through the likes of Behance, there are also a number of marketplaces that you can use to find one. And all kinds of other freelancers for that matter. Some of the ones I have used in the past are Upwork, YunoJuno,

Freelancer and Elance. After you enter your brief, designers from around the world will express an interest in working on your project, for varying fee levels. You'll be able to take a look at their portfolios to see if they've worked on something similar to what you're trying to create. You want to get a sense of the designer's style and try to find someone who is going to 'get' the look and feel you're aiming for.

Because time is of the essence, you may want to use a designer in the opposite time zone to your own, so that they can work on creating your brand while you sleep. So long as you make your deadline clear, you should be able to find a designer who can turn something around in 24 hours.

It goes without saying that this is an extremely quick turnaround, so it will be helpful if your brief and mood board are as specific and easy to understand as possible – you want the designer to hit the nail on the head after just one or two attempts at designing your brand.

Your brief should include the following information to help the designer have the best chance of turning around their work quickly:

Your budget

To avoid wasting your own time or that of the designer, it is a good idea to be totally upfront about your budget. Like anything else in life, the more you are willing to pay, the better the output and the quicker you'll get it back. Having said that, you'd be amazed at the quality of work you can get for just a few hundred pounds – especially if you are able to promise repeat business on the basis of good work.

Timescales

Again, so that the designer you pick knows you're on a tight schedule, be clear what parts of the job you need to be completed by what day and time. Prioritise which parts you need first – most likely the logo – so that you can start incorporating those into the site, while the designer finishes off the rest. In my case, I want to get some promotional materials like cotton tote bags and stickers printed for my launch tomorrow, so I'll need a logo before the end of today – the deadline for next-day printing is 5pm tonight.

THE OBJECTIVE

Explain in very clear and simple terms what the message is you are trying to get across and what specific design items you need – e.g. logo, homepage banners and sign-up icon. Make it clear what you're hoping the consumer will do – e.g. sign up for your subscription, call you for a quote or enter their email address. You should write all of the text yourself, rather than expecting the designer to do this – they're not a mind reader!

Target audience

Your mood board will help massively to convey who your target audience is, but it is also a good idea to explain in words what type of person you are trying to target. This will help the designer to put themselves in their shoes and create something that appeals to them – especially if your target market is very specific.

Any no-nos

There may be specific things that you don't want your design to contain – for example, a colour or word. Make sure you mention these at the start, to avoid having to make extra changes later.

AMAZING OATS DESIGN PROCESS

⏱ Day 1, 2.30pm

Since I want to give customers the message that my oat mixes are 'fun', the best way of doing this on the packaging is to hire an illustrator. I get in touch with Sam Dunn, a freelance illustrator who has worked with many great brands. Her style seems to work well on packaging, and when I explain the need for a quick turnaround, she jumps at the challenge.

I share my mood board with her, a very rough doodle of how I think the label needs to be laid out and the dimensions for the cardboard tube that I have sourced. I send her the barcode images (which I registered very easily through GS1-UK in the UK and can be registered equally easily through the relevant authority in your country), list of ingredients and the nutritional information (which can be calculated with little difficulty for a product like this, since it is simply a pro-rata combination of different components – if your product is more complex, you should take professional advice or ask your supplier).

This process is made so much faster if you give your designers all of the information they need to create the finished designs. If you keep making changes and additions along the way, that's where you can lose a lot of time – and money! Clarity of brief is paramount to getting a quick turnaround.

Sam gets cracking and I ask her to send me examples of what she's working on along the way to be sure that everything is on

track with what I have in mind. Checking in with your designer
every few hours helps to avoid them spending time going down
a path that turns out to be wrong and having to go back and
start again. Within a few hours, and well in time for the 5pm
cut-off deadline for next-day printing, she sends me her idea for
a logo, which I totally love right away.

⏱ Day 1, 4:23pm

Right away, I send the logo off to be printed onto cotton bags
and stickers for the launch tomorrow and Sam gets to work on
creating the actual label designs for my products. After she asks
a few clarifying questions about what information needs to be
visible on the front of the packaging, we end up with a label
design that I think looks great.

It might be a bit lucky to hit a 'hole in one' with your logo
immediately – don't be afraid of doing a few rounds of changes
if it doesn't feel right.

Just to be sure that it's a design that works on the finished
cylindrical tube, Sam does a quick mock-up in Photoshop of
what it will look like – this is an excellent way of ensuring that
your design works in the format that it will eventually end up
being used on.

CHAPTER 6

DOT.COM FROM DAY ONE

🕐 Day 1, 7:30pm

Whether you are selling a physical product, as I am, opening your own bricks-and-mortar store or selling a service, it's absolutely critical that you have a great website. It will always be your biggest 'shop window' into the world and the best opportunity for getting your message across. And the good news is that, even if you don't know the first thing about building a website, you can get something professional online in under a day.

Since I don't know what it is that you are hoping to do with your website, the first step is to be really clear about what is the main thing you want your visitors to be able to do. Most likely it is something pretty standard, like providing information about your opening times, taking bookings or accepting orders. In which case, you will absolutely be able to use one of the fantastic services that are available to build it yourself, without hiring a web designer or a developer.

Where possible, I would definitely recommend this route. Rather than going to the expense and delay of having something custom-built, using something off the shelf gives you the ability to be up and running right away. Building a site from scratch is fraught with difficulties and, like all good building projects, will always take much longer than you initially plan.

There is a huge temptation to believe that your idea is so special and unique that your site needs to be custom-built. So often I meet entrepreneurs who are building some kind of elaborate booking software for their new restaurant concept or an all-singing-all-dancing app for their events business. The reality of course is that most paths have been walked before and there is an off-the-shelf software product to solve most problems that you might be trying to solve.

If you can find an off-the-shelf system, whether to build your site or your app or to run a particular function of your business, I would recommend doing so, at least in the beginning. Even if it doesn't do everything exactly the way you would like, it's better to actually start than to procrastinate trying to build the perfect system.

If doing things this way means that you have to complete certain parts of the process manually, then so be it. What does it matter if some of your process is manual when you don't have many customers? Of course, as your business grows and you are generating funds that you can use to pay expensive developers, you can work on building your own system.

What's more, once you have some experience of what your customers actually want your site to do, you'll be better placed to create a site that works well for them – rather than building features based on your early assumptions about what they want.

In our Beer52 business, we used this approach by initially using Shopify (and a subscription-management plug-in called Chargify) to get our site off the ground in a matter of days, before going on to build our own system from scratch once we knew that what we had come up with was what our customers wanted.

If I haven't managed to convince you to find an off-the-shelf solution to your problems, that's okay. If you really do believe that what you are doing is so unique and complicated that you need to hire a developer, that's absolutely possible to do, and I will share with you some thoughts on how to do that later.

WHAT DOES YOUR SITE NEED TO DO?

Before we jump into the exciting and fun steps of building our sites, we should take a moment to figure out exactly what we want the site to do and, perhaps more importantly, what we want to convince our customers to do from the moment they land on it.

A useful approach to web design is to begin with the creation of a 'wire frame'. This is a very rough sketch of what each page of your site will look like, and how you hope a visitor will flow through it. For example, you will hope that they will go from the homepage to the products page to the basket to the check-out to the payment page.

By putting yourself into the shoes of a visitor to your site, you can figure out what messages you need to present them with on each page and what you hope their action will be at each stage of the journey. Your website is not a piece of art, nor is it just there to give information about your business – it is there to sell your product to people who visit it.

You have to imagine that someone will land on your home-page having never heard anything about you or your business before, and if you can get your messages across in a compelling enough way they will progress through your site, ultimately parting with their credit card details.

A huge number of people won't even stay longer than a few seconds – much in the way that most people will only glance at the labels of products in supermarkets, not taking the time to read more about them. This means that you have to catch their attention very quickly.

People are extremely busy and the internet is full of things that they could be spending their time looking at other than your site. Chances are, they probably have a dozen other tabs open as well as yours. People get extremely annoyed if you waste their time – get to the point!

Make it extremely clear why your product should be in their lives and do it with as little text as possible. Video and quality photography are the best ways of communicating with people on the web – because it takes almost no effort on the part of the viewer to look at a picture, whereas reading a whole page of text is quite frankly a drag, and most people won't bother.

While you're in your customers' shoes, have a think about all of the inevitable questions that are going to spring up in their minds as they look at your site. You must try to address all of these questions snappily and in a way that helps aid the sales process – how much is shipping? Do you deliver internationally? What sizes are available? ('Woo! Delivery is Free!', 'We Delivery Anywhere in Europe', 'Sizes XS–XL Available!').

It seems obvious that you would give these details on your site, but actually most sites fail to be upfront about the boring details. But it is the boring details that people have in their minds, and if you don't tell them the answer they'll just assume the worst – that delivery is expensive and you don't have their size, for example.

In my opinion, the quickest way to figure out what your site should look like is to take inspiration from your competitors' sites. Or perhaps not necessarily competitors' but the site of a business that has had good success online using the same business model as yours.

You can assume that if they have been up and running for some time and are successful, they will have tested and optimised their site to end up with a layout, key messages and design that convert the largest possible number of visitors into customers, which is the name of the game.

GRAZE.COM

When we were first setting up Beer52, we looked for inspiration from great subscription businesses, to get a clue as to how we should design our website. One brand that we got some advice and learned a huge amount from was Graze.com – one of the real pioneers of selling food products on a subscription. As a customer, I love their brand; they send out a cute box with a selection of different healthy treats inside, as frequently as you'd like them to.

The company was founded by a group of entrepreneurs including Graham Bosher, who was also a co-founder of LoveFilm (sold to Amazon for £200m). I knew from having met them that they took a very scientific approach to marketing – testing the conversion on all kinds of different offers, images and website layouts to create a super-optimised offering.

Their success was enormously inspiring and, given that they'd already done years' worth of experimenting by this point, we figured we could learn a lot from them. We looked very closely at how they presented their products on their site, what sort of messages they gave to potential customers and how they encouraged their customers to invite their friends to sign up.

For example, as soon as you land on their site, you are presented with a very clear image of *exactly* what you are going to get when you sign up. This type of photography maybe isn't as 'sexy' as doing something more abstract or including people in the shots, but it helps to communicate exactly to the customer what it is they are being asked to sign up for. It also displays precisely what they are going to pay, rather than hiding that sort of information on a second page.

Their homepage also includes some very clear 'call to action' buttons, which invite the visitor to 'get started'. These are dotted around the page to make sure that, at every point, the potential customer is being encouraged to continue on to the next stage of signing up, rather than getting distracted and moving on to something else.

In very simple terms, the images and illustrations on the site also explain 'how it works', so that there are no doubts in the customer's mind about what exactly this service is and what they're potentially signing up for. Before the brand was a household name, the site also included logos of newspapers and magazines that had featured them, to add credibility.

The clarity of design that Graze pursued is quite striking when you compare it to a lot of other sites, and I think this simplicity partly explains their success in acquiring hundreds of thousands of customers, along, of course, with having a delicious product!

All of these seemingly simple ideas no doubt took a lot of trial and error on Graze's part to come up with. And although what had worked for them wouldn't necessarily work for us, by learning from what they'd created we were not designing our own site completely blind. We had a few clues as to what was likely to be a successful layout and incorporated these with a few of our own ideas to come up with our initial format, which we have since optimised and improved over the years.

CREATING A MOCK-UP

🕐 Day 1, 7:30pm

With the help of this inspiration and with a clear idea of what you want to say and what the basic features of your site should be, it can be helpful to create a mock-up. This is less relevant if you're going to use one of the pre-designed templates that come with the 'DIY' services I'm going to tell you more about, but is very helpful if you plan to hire a developer to build your site from scratch.

One quite simple but useful tool for creating wire frames is Balsamiq Mockups. They offer a free trial, which is all you need since this process is likely to take little more than 15 minutes.

Their software makes it very easy to play around with a site map and individual page layouts, helping you to focus on what the 'big button' needs to be on each page – i.e. the Sign Up or Buy Now buttons.

Once you have created a mock-up, you can either start building your site yourself or send it to your designer/developer if indeed you decide to use one.

DO IT YOURSELF VS HIRING A WEB DEVELOPER

Certainly, if you have no experience of building a website and your idea requires an extremely complicated process, you will have to consider hiring someone to help write the code that runs your site. However, if you are simply looking to sell a product online, without the need for much custom functionality, you can definitely build this yourself, even without any specialist knowledge of coding, software or web development.

What is really exciting to me is that there are now so many tools available online that allow us to get our idea from blank page to web page without having to employ any professional help at all.

A number of services provide a basic template that you can add your own images and text to, creating a very professional-looking website in no time. All you need to do is enter your PayPal account details or another payment processor, such as Stripe, and you can start accepting payments from customers as easily as that.

Shopify

My all-time favourite of these services is Shopify; it's what we've used to build most of SuperJam's sites and we even used it to make the very first version of Beer52. What's particularly cool about it is that, at the click of a button, you can integrate all kinds of 'apps': for advertising, customer service, referrals, and even shipping, tracking and delivery of customers' orders.

SquareSpace

Perfect for a simpler site, SquareSpace can help you very quickly create a beautiful few pages. I'd say this is ideal if you are opening something like a pop-up restaurant or a photography business.

Strikingly

There has been a massive trend recently on the internet towards creating 'one page' sites. These allow the user to scroll down through a series of slides that get a message across in a simple, easy-to-read way. Strikingly has much fewer features than other sites, but that makes it a bit quicker and easier to use. It has great templates for promoting an iPhone app, eBook or other digital products, so if you just need a super-simple webpage, I'd go with them.

CHOOSING A TEMPLATE

A key decision that you will make at this stage is which template to use – this is the basic layout for your site that cannot be changed easily once you commit to it.

Whether you decide to use Strikingly, Shopify or SquareSpace (or any of the many other similar services available), you'll have the option to pick one of their standard free templates, or alternatively to buy a more beautifully designed one from them or via a third party.

🕑 Day 1, 7:42pm

For the Amazing Oats site, I have decided to use Shopify, since it offers the most potential for customisation and add-on features. Although there are many brilliant free templates on their Theme Store, I consider the investment in a premium one to be worthwhile in the long run.

I pick one called 'Maker' from their store and buy it for $180. If you don't want to splash out at this stage, it is absolutely okay to start out with one of the free themes – or you could also check out some of the cheaper Shopify themes on ThemeForest.net.

PHOTOGRAPHY

Photography is perhaps the most important element of any website and, if you have any money at all to invest in your business, this is definitely one of the areas you should spend it on. When people can't physically touch, smell or taste your product, you had better do your best at least to make it look good, as that is all they've got to go on.

It goes without saying that, unless you have a quality camera and a good eye, you shouldn't waste your time trying to photograph your product yourself. You should also be aware that photography and styling are two different skills – some photographers are great at both, but you should definitely consider hiring both a photographer and a stylist if you want some really good images for your site.

You should also know that most photographers specialise in a particular genre – for example fashion, food or still life. Just because someone takes amazing shots of models doesn't mean they will be talented at, or even comfortable with, shooting your homemade cupcakes, for example.

As with anything, the range of prices for a shoot can run from hundreds of pounds to hundreds of thousands of pounds. But you do have a few options to help you achieve more bang for your buck.

First, it is worth doing as much of the groundwork yourself as possible – you should find a suitable location for the shoot (it might just be your own kitchen or garden) as well as sourcing all of the relevant props. In big cities like London, you will be able to find vast prop warehouses that hire out all kinds of interesting objects for shoots by the day – which is much cheaper and quicker than buying them yourself.

Just as when you were briefing the designer for your overall brand, you should create a brief for your photographer. Start by writing a list of all of the exact shots you want to get, whether they should be landscape or portrait, and how they will each be laid out in terms of the props you will be using. It's good to be very clear about what you are expecting from the shoot from the outset – if you start making changes to the brief afterwards, the price your photographer charges will start to creep up too.

To make it really clear to the photographer what you want the images to look like, you should create a mood board, just as for your designer, but this time comprising simply examples of great photography. The images you select should be those you imagine are an easy enough style to recreate and they should all be similar to give the photographer a strong sense of what you are getting at.

A good place to start when looking for a photographer is in your nearest town or city, through Google – most photographers will have an online portfolio that you can view. If they are close by, you'll be able to view the shoot in person and take along all of the props you need to display your product with, which is always best.

Failing that, you can check out some of the online freelance marketplaces – such as PeoplePerHour, Upwork and Elance. With any luck, you will find someone close by that you can work with. If not, depending on what your product is, you might be able to ship it to them on a next-day service for them to photograph. Even with the cost of shipping, if you find a particularly talented photographer in another country who is willing to work for a low fee, you can end up with great work on a low budget.

AMAZING OATS PHOTOSHOOT

🕐 Day 1, 7:42pm

By now, Alex has been working all day on developing the Awesome Oats recipes and he's really pleased with what he has come up with.

He has taken some 'test shots' as a sort of practice before the main shoot tomorrow. We talk through how the finished photography should look. Just as with creating a mood board for my designer, I provide a 'reference shot'; an image that we can try to recreate in our own style. I really love the brand Mast Brothers and think that their abstract, geometric photography really helps to sell their luxury chocolate. I send a few of their images to Alex so that he gets the idea of what I'm talking about.

We agree that all of the shots should include the finished packaging design. As soon as we have a label design, we'll get some printed off at a print shop near his house and attached to the cardboard tubes from Visican tomorrow.

I explain that what I'll need for the site are a few 'lifestyle' shots of the finished porridge product, showing people how it will look once they've prepared it themselves, alongside the packaging. What's important is to use photography online to explain the product in a way that you would if you had the opportunity to show it to your customers in real life. Use it to really bring it to life. As well as these lifestyle shots, I'll need some 'straight on' images of the packaging to show in the 'shop' area of my online store.

All-in, the photo shoot will cost around £500 for professionally styled images of my products. I personally think that great photography offers the best return on investment for any business; if you consider that your website is your shop window, dressing it well is your best chance to develop sales.

STOCK PHOTOGRAPHY

But if you don't want to make this sort of investment of time and money in commissioning a photoshoot, as I have done, you may consider using some of the excellent stock photography that is available online. Maybe your business just needs some high-quality general images related to your product or service to help bring your website to life.

Through sites such as Shutterstock, Alamy, iStockphoto and Dreamstime, you can browse millions of images that are available to license for your own purposes. These can be fairly inexpensive and offer you an extremely quick way of getting great images onto your site.

VIDEO

If your product is particularly technical or you feel that it needs some explanation, you might decide to do this with an 'intro video' – a quick clip on the homepage of a website that succinctly explains what you are all about. Video is perhaps the most engaging way to communicate your message online – so long as you do it in the right way.

As with photography, your budget will drastically affect the quality of the output. In an ideal world, you will have the budget to pay for a cameraperson, soundperson and video editor. However, given you're most likely on a tighter budget than that, you should be able to find one person who can do all three well enough to create a decent video for your site.

You can find your filmmaker in much the same way as finding a photographer: by checking out freelancer marketplaces and portfolio listing sites. It will be best if you write the script for the video yourself, since nobody knows your story and product better than you do. Make sure that you get to the point – don't waste your viewers' time – most people will only watch the first few seconds of your video and, if you bore them, they'll stop right there.

Use your video to get your main message across – don't go into every technical detail. If people want more info, that's what your website is for. Probably the most successful (and most aped) intro video of all time was for DollarShaveClub.com. In that video, the company's founder explains their product in such an entertaining and compelling way that they received many millions of shares on social media.

'Doing a Dollar Shave Club' is much easier than it sounds – the reality is that there are a lot of talented people working hard to create viral videos. It's unlikely that you'll be so lucky that an advert for your product will spread like wildfire. But what you can do is learn from those success stories about what makes a good video: short, to the point, usually funny and, most importantly, original.

Simply copying someone else's video or creating something low grade will do your brand more harm than good. I would suggest only creating a video if you think you can do something of good quality. This is the reason I don't plan on making a video for Awesome Oats; I simply don't think I have the time, nor do I think it's necessary for such a simple product.

FIVERR.COM

In one of the stranger corners of the internet lies a site called Fiverr. Here, people post examples of things they are willing to do for just five dollars. You will be surprised by what people are able and willing to do for almost nothing.

It is in fact possible to hire professional voiceover artists, puppeteers and even models, to create short videos describing your product. Needless to say, for only a few pounds you're not going to win any Oscars, but you could well create something reasonably professional or use one of these services to put the finishing touches onto your video clip.

I'd say that Fiverr is perfect if you are creating a brand that doesn't take itself too seriously and you have given yourself some creative space to fool around in. You could hire someone dressed as a monkey to endorse your product on camera, to write your brand across their forehead or perhaps incorporate it into a funny song.

REVIEWS

As soon as possible, you will want your site to contain real reviews from customers, the press or any experts in your industry. If there's anyone that you can get a quote from right away, this is something that will add a huge amount of credibility to your otherwise completely unknown brand.

There are various review apps that plug in nicely to the Shopify platform and the best ones are those that allow people to comment using Facebook. People are much less likely to write spam or abuse if their comment is connected to their real identity. They're also much more likely to 'like' your product if you make it really easy for them to do so.

Collecting people's reviews using a third-party app such as the one we use at Beer52, called Trustpilot, adds an extra layer of credibility to your site. It's extremely important that people trust your brand – especially when they have never heard of it – so these type of programs can really help, as long as your product is good enough actually to get good reviews in the first place!

MAILING LIST

I'd say that basically every business should have an email newsletter; you should never pass on the opportunity to collect customers' email addresses. Someone might well have an interest in your business but not necessarily place an order right away. By keeping them up to date with improvements, new products and other news as your business develops, their initial interest may well convert into a sale a little further down the line.

There are lots of very easy apps, such as MailChimp, which allow you to set up a simple email capture box on your site. These link up very easily with Shopify and the other website-building platforms, so this super-simple marketing technique definitely shouldn't be overlooked.

If you really want to boost your email marketing list, you could set up a 'pop-up' on your homepage, offering potential customers 10 per cent off their first order if they let you know their email address. Simply include a discount code in the automated welcome email that they'll be sent by the program.

LIVE CHAT

One of the lovely features of services like Shopify is that you can integrate live chat services into your site – some of these are even free. Zopim and Olark are a couple of examples, but there are many more with a variety of features, so shop around and find the one that is right for your site.

These services provide a little pop-up box at the bottom of your site that allows a visitor to enter questions about your product. You or someone else can then answer them and walk them through the whole sales process, hopefully increasing the percentage of people who go on to buy.

In the early days of starting out, it can be extremely helpful to give customers this opportunity to ask you questions right there on the homepage. You'll quickly realise what parts of your message are not getting across, what is causing confusion and what additional information you need to include to hopefully increase your conversion rate (that is to say, the number of visitors who go on to buy anything from you).

CONTACT FORMS

Similarly, you can create an excellent contact form using services such as Wufoo. This service allows you to create a form with numerous options, buttons and drop-down menus. This will allow you to capture lots of information from prospective customers when they get in touch with a question, inquiry or booking. It is also worth just having a contact email address available on the site, as some people prefer not to use contact forms and you definitely don't want to miss out on any leads just because of that.

FREQUENTLY ASKED QUESTIONS

To minimise the number of repetitive, simple questions that people will contact you about over and over again, make sure that your site has a detailed FAQ page right from the start. By having as much information on your site as possible, you will help to alleviate any of the fears or concerns that people may have, which could otherwise stop them from ordering.

This page should cover all of the boring details that you don't want to cover on the sexier pages of your site – like, what happens if my delivery doesn't show up? Can I track my order online? Where do your ingredients come from? Are you hiring?

A nice app for creating this page is the Desk.com customer support service. It will help you to populate an FAQ page with lots of questions and will also create Q&As based on dialogues that you have with customers over time. What's really cool is that it will help you to manage your interactions with customers across all of the different contact points they may have with your brand: email, phone, Facebook, Twitter and so on.

SUBSCRIPTION PAYMENTS

For Beer52 and perhaps your business too, it is necessary to process recurring subscription payments each month, which comes with a number of challenges. Inevitably, customers' payments will fail, their cards will expire over time, they will want to cancel their payments and also skip months here and there, when they go on holiday for example.

The good news is that there are a number of services available that remove all of these headaches – by managing this process for you, in exchange for a small fee. The ones that I recommend are Chargify (which integrates nicely with Shopify), Saasy or Spreedly. Which one is best will depend on your country, merchant bank account and payment processor, so be sure to check out all of your options before committing to one.

You should check out GoCardless, which is a system for letting people pay by Direct Debit – much cheaper to process than credit or debit cards, and there's also a much lower rate of payments failing.

PAYMENT PROCESSING

If you are not accepting subscriptions, the payment processing will be extremely simple. All you need to do is set up a free account with, for example, PayPal or Stripe, and enter your account details into the Payments section of Shopify. When a customer checks out of your online store, they will automatically pay what they owe you into your PayPal account. Then you just need to get PayPal to transfer your funds into your bank account – easy!

If, like me, you are planning to accept payments on an ongoing subscription basis, you will need to set up both a merchant bank account and a payment gateway. The best ones to use vary by country, so check with Chargify or whichever subscription-management system you are using.

OFFLINE PAYMENTS

Some start-ups will need to be able to accept credit card payments in the 'real world', for example if you are selling your products at live events, parties or even door to door.

The quickest and easiest way of doing this is to set up an account with Square, iZettle, or one of the numerous other mobile-based payment processors. With a nifty little gadget that you attach to your phone or tablet, you can start swiping cards right away, accepting payments of any amount wherever you are.

AWESOME OATS WEBSITE DEVELOPMENT

⏱ Day 1, 8:10pm

Having opened an account with a free 14-day trial from Shopify, chosen a theme that I like and installed it to my account, I'm ready to get going. I start by adding my logo and writing a little about the story of how I came up with the idea for Awesome Oats. I add a photo of myself to the 'About' page – I absolutely recommend doing this; not only does including your own personal story give your brand some authenticity, it helps people to trust you.

I don't have finished product photographs to upload just yet, but I can complete almost everything else on my site. I stay up late linking my domain name to my site, adding my terms and conditions and adding all of the basic information about my business such as my phone number and address.

⏱ Day 1, 10:17pm

SET UP A COMPANY EMAIL ADDRESS

Using the control panel for your new domain name, you'll be able to set up a forwarding 'catchall' that will send all emails sent to that address to your existing email account. It is best that you use Gmail, so that you can easily configure it to be able to reply from that domain name too (i.e. when I email someone, it'll show fraser@awesomeoats.com in the 'from' field. If you're not sure how to do this, just google 'how to set up a catchall email with …' and include the name of your domain provider.

REGISTER A PHONE NUMBER

I recommend setting up a Skype number (this looks like a normal landline phone number but actually diverts calls to your Skype account). You can pick a number for virtually any country in the world, so you can appear to be based in, for example, the UK, but actually be working from the beach in Spain.

⏱ Day 1, 10:46pm

WRITE YOUR SITE'S TERMS AND CONDITIONS

It is really important that your site has a complete list of T&Cs: Returns Policy, Privacy Policy, Cookies Policy, Data Protection Statement, Contact Details and details of which Governing Law your site is subject to. Rather than writing these out from scratch, you can very easily find a template online or even just rephrase your competitors' terms, which will be publicly displayed on their website. Or, you can use a tool called TermsFeed to help you do it.

And now it's time to get some sleep. I'm exhausted but delighted that in just one day I have come up with an idea for a business, given it a name and hired both an illustrator and a food stylist to help me bring it to life. What's more, I've set up the basics of my website ready to add my finished product tomorrow.

Good night!

CHAPTER 7

FINDING YOUR FIRST CUSTOMER

The ways that you can promote your business are endless, and no doubt you already have some ideas of your own by this point. Over the years, in the businesses that I have been involved in, we have tried all kinds of different methods of getting our name out there. In this chapter I want to share with you some of those that have worked best for us, what I've learned from them, and how you can use them to attract your first few customers.

With Awesome Oats, I will try to find different types of customers – one retail store and some online customers – to give you an idea of how you can approach those two different channels. Of course, what is likely to work best for your business will depend very much on what you are selling, so I will also touch on a few other channels that you might find lucrative.

CRAFT MARKETS

If you are making a product at home, just as I am, a super-obvious place to start is to find out about your local craft fairs and farmers' markets. These can be a great test-bed for your new product and usually don't cost that much to participate in. Simply get in touch with the organisers, and let them know a bit about your products and why you think you will be able to bring something new and exciting to their market.

They will usually want to make sure that you have a food hygiene certificate – you can actually complete the necessary training online and print off the relevant documentation quite easily. Your premises will probably also need to be inspected by a government official and you will need as well to provide a copy of your public liability insurance. In the UK, by joining the 'National Market Traders Federation' you will be covered by their insurance policy and qualify for various other benefits.

My advice would be to invest in creating an attractive stand – maybe get a cloth banner printed with your logo on it, along with some tote bags and fliers about your brand. Invest in some attractive wooden crates or other furnishings to display your product in an interesting way.

FACEBOOK

Unless you're one of the few strange people who doesn't have a Facebook account, you probably already have some idea about how Facebook advertising works. Based on people's 'likes' and other data, advertisers such as you and me can show ads for our products to groups of people that we think are most likely to buy them.

Setting up a campaign is very easy; you can literally have something online, being displayed to prospective customers, within minutes. When you set up your campaign, Facebook will invite you to define how targeted you want your ad to be. You can select the location, age and gender of your target customer and then also select which pages you think they already like.

My advice would be to start out as targeted as possible – there's a temptation to cast your net too wide, but it's actually quality over quantity that counts with this type of campaign. Given that you're just trying to get your first few customers, it's a good idea to show your ads to people who are genuinely likely to buy – otherwise you'll be pouring money down the drain. Target people whose 'likes' show an interest in your competitors' products, in the overall thrust of your business, or maybe in complementary products.

The only other thing left to do is to upload some eye-catching images that really sell what you're trying to do. I suggest uploading as many different images as you can and then closely monitoring which ones perform the best – it can often surprise you!

Once you have built up a good customer database, you can use Facebook's 'Lookalike Audience' feature to serve your adverts to people whose profile is similar to that of others who have bought from you in the past. We always find that this works well, so long as you have a reasonably large database of previous customers.

GOOGLE

Just as with advertising on Facebook, you can use Google AdWords to target your customers with high precision. What's different about Google is that people are actively looking for something, so you're potentially putting your ad in front of them at exactly the right moment.

It's important when you pick your keywords for Google to make sure that you can actually deliver on what you promise. If I were to advertise on the keyword 'muesli', for example, when people landed on my site they'd immediately leave since porridge wasn't what they were looking for.

It also helps if you can set up individual pages for each keyword, so that when a customer lands on your site they're presented with something completely relevant to what they searched for. For example, if someone were to search for 'banana porridge', they'd land directly on the page that shows my banana porridge.

This all sounds obvious enough but it can become relatively complicated to manage your AdWords on a big scale. Once you have used your campaigns to attract your first few customers, you may well find it worthwhile to hire a freelancer to optimise your keywords and landing pages. It's not uncommon to be bidding on hundreds, even thousands, of different combinations of keywords at any one time. You will have selected the keywords that you think are relevant and, whenever someone searches for those terms, an instantaneous auction takes place; the brand that has offered the most money to advertise on the search results of those terms will win the space.

RETARGETING

One of the most cost-effective forms of online advertising I have come across is retargeting. This is where your site places a cookie onto the browser of people who are visiting your site. When they then go elsewhere on the internet, for example to the *New York Times* or the *Guardian* websites, an advert for your site will be on display. Since they have clearly already shown an interest in your product by visiting your site in the past, there is a fair chance that if you remind them of your products they'll come back and perhaps buy the second time around.

One of the biggest providers of retargeting ad placements is AdRoll, whose system you can easily integrate into your site – especially if you are using Shopify. Just like with Google and Facebook advertising, you will pay for this on a per-click basis, entering the maximum you would be willing to pay for a click, how much you are willing to spend per day and letting the system do the rest.

GROUP-BUYING SITES

In every country, there are countless group-buying sites that you could use to launch your business. By offering a really good deal, you will not only expose your brand to thousands of subscribers of that site's mailing list; you will also hopefully be able to attract your first few hundred customers. Even if you don't make much money from the initial sale, you should be able to make money from repeat business.

Usually, the group-buying site (like Groupon, LivingSocial or Wowcher) works off a margin of anywhere between 10 and 35 per cent, just like any other retailer. However, they expect to be able to offer your product for around 50 per cent off the regular retail price, so, working back from that, you'll need to figure out if it's even possible to discount your prices that aggressively and still make money.

How these sites make their money is from 'non-redemptions', that is to say the people who buy a voucher and never use it. When you're negotiating your deal with them, you should make sure that you get a share of this – a lot of vendors don't know anything about it and miss out on a lot of revenue as a result.

LINKEDIN

Depending on what you are selling, you may be able to find customers by using LinkedIn. By upgrading to a premium account (which you can do for one month for free), you will be able to search for possible prospects and contact them either through the site or, preferably, by guessing their email address (it's usually something like firstname.lastname@companyname. com).

LinkedIn also has an advertising platform, which would be useful if you are selling a product or service for the corporate market. LinkedIn groups and events can be used to promote what you're up to.

PRE-SALES

I come across a lot of smart designers who create a prototype of a product very quickly and then, before committing to the first production run out of their own pocket, wait until they find 1,000 people – or however many they need to cover the minimum first production run that their third-party manufacturer demands – to place advanced orders. This way, they know that their product is sold before taking the risk of producing it.

You might think that this model would annoy consumers, by making them wait a long time for their delivery (or potentially not even delivering it at all, since, if insufficient pre-orders are made, the designer might decide to scrap the project entirely and refund those who've ordered). But what's amazing is that they actually tend to think it's kind of cool – to be supporting a new product into existence, helping a new designer get their idea off the ground and, of course, being one of the first people in the world to own it. It seems that the inconvenience of having to wait a long time for delivery is far outweighed by the novelty of being first.

There are lots of companies that have successfully built their entire business on this model. One good example is Made.com in the UK. They design 'high street style' furniture but sell it online at a discount, not having to pay the considerable overheads of having physical city-centre showrooms for their customers to view the furniture they're buying.

It might amaze you that people are willing to order something like a sofa over the internet without actually seeing it but, remarkably, they are – and they're even willing to wait a few months for it to show up. Some online furniture companies don't produce the furniture until they've got enough orders to produce a batch and ship it economically in containers all in one go.

KICKSTARTER

It is absolutely conceivable that you could launch a Kickstarter campaign to raise the necessary funds for your business idea in 48 hours. In case you're not familiar with the model, how it works is that you create a page for your idea and invite strangers to contribute funds towards helping to make it happen. In exchange for backing your project, you offer them something in return – a lifetime membership, one of the first editions or just one of your products as soon as it becomes available.

What's cool about this model is that, not only can you crowd-fund your idea, but you can generate an army of fans of it who can help in all kinds of other ways. Of course, once someone has pledged money, in a sense they have a vested interest in seeing your concept become a success – which means they will no doubt share it with their friends, send in ideas for what they think you should do and ultimately become loyal customers in the long term.

Nothing is more powerful than an idea whose time has come, says an old adage. And in the case of Kickstarter campaigns, if you happen to have hit upon a timely idea, you can see it propelled into stratospheric levels of success at incredible speed. Many entrepreneurs have been known to raise millions of dollars in funding for their projects in a matter of hours.

PRESS RELEASES

I can't tell you how important media coverage has been to the success of SuperJam. The hundreds of interviews that I have done with newspapers, magazines, radio stations and TV shows have definitely helped to turn the brand into what it is today.

You can't just pay journalists to write about your product – not in most countries anyway. You have to have a story that journalists want to write about and their readers want to read about. There's no magic secret to getting your story out there. In my case, we have never sent out a press release and rarely hired a PR agency. Whenever we have tried doing things that way, it's totally flopped. I'm sure there are some fine PR agencies around, and perhaps you'll be able to find them, but unless you have a good story in the first place, there's only so much they can do.

Journalists are incredibly pressed for time, so if you do plan on pitching your story to them, it's your job to make writing about your business as easy as possible. You should literally write the article yourself – the headline, subline, some quotes from other people related to your story – giving details at the bottom of who they can contact for further quotes or info. If you can supply them with some pictures too, that saves them sending out their photographer.

If you are working in a particular niche industry, you maybe don't care so much about national media coverage. What you might be more interested in is coverage within your sector's trade press. If that's the case, don't be afraid of looking up which journalists write about your particular field in the right publications and contact them directly with your story. Their name is usually credited alongside their articles, so it shouldn't be that hard to email them!

BLOGGERS

For any type of product, there are thousands of bloggers out there who could be interested in writing about it. Generally, they're small-time writers creating content out of a passion for their subject, rather than as a money-making venture. So, chances are, they'll be delighted with some free stuff.

With all of the businesses I have been involved with, we've created huge lists of all of the bloggers we think could be relevant for our brand and just sent them a friendly email telling them about what we're up to, and offering a free sample if they're interested in writing about us or reviewing our product.

Usually, they reply right back saying they're happy to do so, and before you know it we've got a nice dialogue going with someone who's just as passionate about our industry as we are.

So long as you are confident about the quality of your product, you should feel happy to send out free samples to bloggers and journalists. Of course, they're not obliged to write nice things about you, but if your product is as good as it should be they'll write a glowing review that links to your site and brings in traffic. These links will also help to boost your ranking on Google, which is really important.

Just be sure to follow up with them after they've tried your samples, and send them lots of information and photographs to make writing an informative, interesting blog post really easy. And whenever you have new stories in the future, keep them in the loop, as there is a fair chance they'll be happy to write follow-up articles about your story as things develop.

FREE SAMPLES

Giving out free samples of your products is one of the simplest ways of creating some buzz. Everyone is happy to take a freebie and, more often than not, if your product is any good they'll be tempted to buy. I know that I'm a sucker for free samples – I always politely take the freebie at the supermarket but then feel obliged to buy the product the person is promoting. Even I fall for this stuff, and I spend all day coming up with these kinds of tricks!

If it wasn't for handing out the freebies, most people would never have noticed the product in the first place. So long as it doesn't cost too much to let someone try your product for free, you should always carry samples to give out to people you meet. Everyone is a potential customer!

I once read that William Wrigley, the founder of the eponymous chewing gum empire, established himself by sending a free packet of chewing gum to everyone listed in the American phone books, one and a half million people or so. Of course, a lot of them got in touch to buy his product at full price after they sampled it – and the rest is history.

Partly inspired by that story, I thought it would be fun to give away a vast number of jars of SuperJam to see what would happen. So, a few years ago, we gave away a free jar of SuperJam to every reader of the *Sun* newspaper, which cost me nothing more than the free samples themselves. Newspapers are more than happy to distribute free samples because, by offering something for free to people buying their paper, they can sell more copies.

So we had a coupon printed on the front page of the paper offering readers a free jar of SuperJam if they took the coupon to one of our stockists. The *Sun* is the biggest-selling newspaper in the English-speaking world. Something like five and a half million people read it every day and I found myself on the front page of the Susan Boyle Special Edition of the paper – undoubt-edly my proudest moment as a Scottish person!

Needless to say, we ran out of jam that day and tens of thou-sands of free jars were distributed to people who, in all likeli-hood, had never heard of our brand up until that point. Sales in the weeks after the experiment took a significant step up, so the tactic certainly seemed to work.

I repeated the offer a few more times, experimenting with all kinds of different newspapers and magazines and favouring those with the best response rates; in total, we printed more than fifty million coupons in newspapers and women's magazines. They had a face value of tens of millions of pounds and so it was definitely a scary time; I was worried that one day everyone would take their coupons to the supermarkets to get free jam and we wouldn't have enough money to pay for it!

By running all of these promotions in the national press, we were able to introduce the SuperJam brand to millions of people and, since we were using coupons, we could measure how effec-tive it was. As we would use a unique coupon for each advert, we could track which newspapers and offers were sending us the most customers based on the number of coupons that ended up being redeemed. In the end, we could see that the promotions brought with them a huge uplift in sales and the cost of running them was quickly covered.

As well as giving away free samples via newspapers and maga-zines, you can also literally stand in the stores getting people to try your products. If you're starting out with a stall at a farmers' market, make sure you've got plenty of free tasters to hand out to passers-by.

PRINT ADVERTISING

There's an old saying about print advertising, which is that one out of ten pounds you spend on it will be worth it – and the problem is that you don't know which one. It is undoubtedly not a cheap way to promote your start-up business – most well-known publications won't entertain a budget of anything less than at least a grand. And, for the best results, you probably want to invest in a spread of placements across a number of publications, lowering the risk that the newspaper or magazine you've chosen isn't the right one for your brand.

Generally, people will pay most attention to editorials, skipping the adverts wherever they can – so the best types of column inches are those you get for free. When you pay for advertising, most people won't look at your ad and your product may well only be relevant to a small proportion of those who do.

Despite these challenges, a lot of successful companies have been built on the back of print advertising. And there's a lot to be said for promoting your brand to a targeted audience of interested consumers, through a specialist niche publication.

I have picked up a number of lessons and a lot of advice from people about this old-school form of promotion, which hopefully will be useful to anyone wanting to use print advertising to promote their business from day one.

One of the best ways to learn about successful print advertising is to take note of the ads that appear repeatedly in the same publications. There will no doubt be ads that you recognise as having been in your face a hundred times before. These are usually direct response, or mail order, ads – the 'call now' or 'use this special code for a discount'-type ads. They tend to be selling some boring or wacky product that isn't on sale in normal shops. They're usually not sexy, they never win design awards and they're loaded with way more text than the more common 'brand-building'-style adverts for products such as toothpaste or dog food. But the thing you can be sure of is that they work — the direct response advertiser knows afterwards exactly how many sales a particular ad placement generated (for example, by using a special phone number for each advert, or a unique discount code that allows them to track how many online sales can be directly attributed to that ad). If one particular magazine is no good for them, they don't advertise again.

Such adverts are also the original A/B split-testers. A direct response advertiser will run two versions of the same ad — perhaps with different headlines — and see which one gets the most sales. By constantly tweaking and testing their ad layout and copy, they end up creating a highly optimised ad that they know gets results.

So, based on this knowledge, we can see that the types of ads that get instant results aren't those with a picture of a beautiful girl posing next to a product. They're the ones that look almost exactly like normal articles — direct response ads have loads of text, photography that explains very clearly what the function of the product is and, above all, a focus on exactly why people should buy it and why they should buy it *today*.

A word of warning, though: as well as being potentially an expensive experiment with no guaranteed results, a badly designed advert can do more harm than good. As with your website, packaging and everything else that your customers see, I recommend strongly that you invest as much as you can afford in hiring an experienced designer to create an advert that looks good and does a great job of getting your message across.

To tell the truth, I have never believed in investing huge amounts of money in print advertising for any of the businesses I have been involved with — there are lots of other forms of advertising that are much more measurable and have a far smaller impact on your starting budget. One of the problems with print ads is that it's usually hard to test them with small amounts of money, before scaling up your spending when you know you have a design that sells.

But that isn't always the case. Sometimes it is possible to negotiate a 'cost per acquisition' deal with a newspaper or magazine. That's to say that for every customer they send your way, you'll pay them a commission. This means there's no risk for you and the newspaper can make some revenue out of some ad space that they otherwise weren't going to sell for a fixed price.

Another potentially low-risk way of running print advertising is to focus on a specialist magazine or newspaper that a lot of your target customers read. Perhaps you believe that it might be a good place to promote the launch of your business, since it is so targeted to the type of people you need to go after, thereby reducing the risk of failure. You can also always haggle on the price of print advertising, and many publications offer a special discount to first-time advertisers.

When you come to create your ad, you should have a clear idea in your head about what the message is that you are trying to get across – essentially, why should someone buy from you right now? If it isn't clear to you, it's even less clear to the reader.

Rather than screaming your message in people's faces, try to create an ad that is interesting – think about what makes you read normal editorial copy. An eye-catching and intriguing headline, interesting photography, and testimonials from existing customers all help. You are an expert at what you do, so it should be easy for you to write an ad that makes people understand your passion and what sets you apart from everyone else.

For your 48-hour start-up, it is unrealistic to expect your advert to be printed in papers or magazines in such a short space of time, but you could definitely write and design the ad and negotiate your first placements for it in a matter of hours. My advice would be to create a direct-response-style ad. Even though it isn't glamorous, you'll be able to measure exactly how much money you made from each placement, giving you valuable lessons to improve your ad and choice of publications in the future. And, as a start-up with limited funds, you really want to create adverts that pay off quickly and get results.

DIRECT MAIL

Aside from standing in the street with a sandwich board to promote your new venture, there probably isn't any kind of advertising less romantic than direct mail. It conjures up images of all the junk that gets indiscriminately posted through our letter-boxes every day – the pizza shops, taxi companies and landscape gardeners scattering their name all over town in the hope that someone might read their poorly designed, cheaply printed flier and go to the effort of picking up the phone to find out more.

Although it definitely isn't a sexy way to promote your new business, a well-designed, targeted direct mail campaign can prove to be a successful method of finding your vital first few customers. It's not right for every new company, but it is well suited to a business that is targeting customers in a specific geographical area. It can also be ideal if you're aiming to sell to a specific type of company – for example, if you're launching a new pet product, you might want to send a sample or information directly to every pet shop in the country.

Designing a direct mail campaign

When you're thinking about how to design a piece of direct mail, in my opinion you need to be totally aware of the extent to which you're imposing yourself on your customer. They really didn't expect to hear from you and, quite honestly, don't have any interest in your promotion. Just sending them some advertising about your business out of the blue in the post is pretty rude, when you think about it.

So, if you want people to take the time to pay attention to what you've got to say, you'd better design something that is exciting and interesting. Better yet, if you send something that is actually useful people are far less likely just to throw it in the bin. Make it super-clear to people what you want them to do, now that they've heard about you – are you giving them a special deal if they go online or ring to place an order in the next seven days? If you can create a sense of urgency, the person reading your message will hopefully do something about it right away; otherwise they'll forget all about it and you'll have lost a potential customer.

Your direct mail materials are your first impression, so it's worth investing the necessary money in making them as beautiful and as engaging as possible. Think about how you can get your message across in a fun and intriguing way that isn't just shouting in people's faces.

I personally hardly receive any physical mail any more, and most people only receive things they hate – spam and bills for the most part. So if you can design your campaign well, there can be something exciting about receiving a surprise in the post. In the age of Facebook, there's something genuinely special about a friend taking the time to send you a postcard or a handwritten letter. A good direct mail campaign should aim to capture some of that magic.

Converting your promotion into sales

If you have sent your potential customers a piece of direct mail or perhaps a sample of your product, you need to follow that up with a phone call the next day. Ask them what they thought of your offer. A good combination of direct mail and telesales can hit the sweet spot – if it's done in the right way, your follow-up phone call can successfully tip the balance into someone placing an order with you.

Whether you plan on phoning your customers or not, your direct mail campaign should lead people to an exact online location. You can create a landing page specifically for those who respond to your promotion – for instance www.yourwebsite. com/campaign. This page should aim to answer all of the questions that people will have at this point and then give them the opportunity to try your product or service at a special rate, using a discount code that you have printed on your marketing materials. This will also help you to track conversions – so you know exactly how many new customers your campaign has brought in – otherwise you won't know how successful it has been and whether or not you should run a similar promotion again in the future.

TARGETED MARKETING

Sending marketing to people in the post obviously costs a huge amount more per person than email, which is essentially free. This means, for it to succeed, you have to do everything you can to avoid wasting money through posting to people who are never going to buy from you.

The more targeted your campaign is, the higher the conversion rate will be in terms of the number of people who go on to place an order. The conversion rate is the magic number in this type of marketing and you want to do everything you can to increase it. Using quality, up-to-date data to target your campaign to the right people is what is going to make the biggest difference.

When planning any form of direct marketing, it is important to make sure that your promotions and data-gathering comply with the law. You can get some guidance on this via the Information Commissioner's website.

BUYING DATA

I touched on this earlier in the book and there are a number of ways that you can get the names and addresses of your potential customers. One of the easiest, although potentially not the cheapest, options is by buying a database from Royal Mail (the postal service in most countries offers a similar service).

They will be able to sell you a database of consumer addresses based on a number of criteria – for example, you might want to send your mailing to people who have recently moved home or who live in a house worth more than a million.

If you're trying to sell your product to businesses, it's really easy to buy a database of all of the pet shops, ice-cream shops or garden centres in the country. This is because, when someone incorporates their company, they have to select what type of business it is, and this information is made publicly available. For very little money, you can have a complete list of all of your prospective customers, ready for you to contact with your great offer.

TEST MARKETING CAMPAIGN

As with our initial customer testing at the start of the book, a good tip before doing a large campaign is to test any potential data source for its quality. Whether you are getting these potential customers' details from another brand or a specialist agency, they should be able to give you a random sample of their database. You can run a small campaign for, say, 50 or 500 people, depending on what is relevant for your promotion to check the accuracy of their information.

As with all kinds of promotions, it's a good idea to run a small campaign before you wade in and bet the farm on an unproven method. Carefully track the conversions that come from your first mailing to figure out exactly how much money you have made. If you have made more in profit than the cost of the mail-out, it's probably worth running it on a bigger scale. Otherwise, you'll need to figure out what you can change about the design or targeting to improve the conversion rate.

EMAIL MARKETING

Your direct mail campaign might actually have nothing to do with putting fliers through letter-boxes – it may well be completely digital.

A relatively cheap and obvious way to promote your start-up is via email marketing. However, in a world where most people receive hundreds of emails a day, most of them spam and most deleted without a glance, you're going to have to put some thought into what you can do to get people actually to read your message.

Just as with buying mailing addresses, it is possible to buy targeted email databases for people or companies. You can then simply upload the data into MailChimp or another bulk email service to send out your promotion. Be careful that it's not too spammy, because if more than 2 per cent of recipients mark it as spam, you'll have a hard time being allowed to send out future campaigns.

You can also pay an existing email newsletter to carry your promotion, which is perfect if you're aiming your product at a special interest group, like professional athletes or beekeepers. You can offer the owner of that list a commission on each of the customers their email campaign sends your way.

Whether you are sending your sales email to one person or 10,000, you should try to personalise each and every one for the individual who is reading it. The more you can do to customise your offer to the particular customer you are targeting, the more likely they are to buy from you, it's as simple as that.

What's clever about email marketing is that you can automatically generate a completely unique email for each of your potential customers – by using the information that you know about them. You may know what products they have browsed on your store, what area they live in or how old they are – all useful pieces of information that can help you create an email that is as specific as possible to the person receiving it.

Make your email message short and snappy. Be very clear about what you want the other person to do. Are you asking for their feedback on your product? Do you want them to take advantage of your special offer?

If you don't know the email address for the company you're trying to reach, a useful tip is to know that info@ almost always reaches the person who is in charge of the company's website – which in a small business will also be the person in charge of marketing, maybe even the owner of the business.

TELESALES

Just the word 'telesales' is probably enough to send a shiver down your spine. In fact, I haven't met many people who enjoyed picking up the phone, dialling numbers and trying to sell a product to the person at the other end.

I myself really used to hate calling customers on the phone – I felt like I was probably being rude by interrupting their day to try to sell my product to them. But, unfortunately, it is often the case that there's no better way of getting through to someone than just picking up the phone and calling them. And if your whole business relies on getting through to that person – if you're trying to sell to the buyer of a big retailer, for example – then you may just have to go ahead and overcome your fear.

Just as in all kinds of direct marketing, I believe in taking a scientific and measurable approach to telesales. Start by writing a basic script that you think is likely to work: a reason for why you are calling today, what your offer is and a question that invites your potential customer to say something other than yes or no.

As you talk to more and more customers, you'll get a sense of what works and what doesn't; keep tweaking your script, testing different things and improving your offer until you have something that delivers. You'll be surprised by how much you can improve your performance between your first call and your fiftieth. And as your pitch starts working, your confidence will improve and you'll start to feel completely comfortable picking up the phone.

TRADE FAIRS

Over the years, one of the best ways we've met new stockists for SuperJam and promoted the brand to consumers has been at big events like trade shows, music festivals and food fairs. You may well find out about an event that you feel would be ideal for your brand and decide to set up a stall there, showing your brand off to the possibly thousands of people who come along. You can take the opportunity to hand out samples, promotional materials and maybe collect people's contact details by offering a prize draw.

For whatever product you are selling, whether it is toothpaste, recycling services or furniture, there are trade shows all around the world where everyone from your industry will come together for a couple of days to show off their wares. They can be a great place to do some research about the market, meet potential customers or 'shop' your competitors – posing as a potential customer to get an insight into their sales process and special offers, which you may want to take some inspiration from for your own business.

You don't necessarily need to hire a stand to get the most out of trade shows – if all of your potential customers are at an exhibition together, why not just go there and introduce your-self to them at their stand. Sure, this can be a little cheeky, trying to sell your product to them when they've paid for the chance to sell theirs at this particular event, but meeting them face to face is a golden opportunity. And having them all lined up in an exhibition hall for you to meet should be like shooting fish in a barrel!

Attending events and trade fairs is also a brilliant way of meeting other entrepreneurs and companies that are operating in a similar field to you. You can talk shop with them; find out where they sell their products and who you should be speaking to as well. You might even find that you can form partnerships with other companies to help each other find new customers.

If you do decide to invest in having your own stand at an exhibition, I've found that having something exciting going on at your installation or booth at a show can draw hundreds of people towards your brand. Whether that is a cookery demon-stration, an unusual stand design, free samples or just free beer, try doing something different to set you apart from the hundreds of other stands that will be there.

It goes without saying that you should make an effort to collect people's business cards or contact details, so that you can follow up with a phone call or a meeting and hopefully win their business. If they remember meeting you at the event, the chances are they'll be happier to talk to you than if you were just someone calling out of the blue.

In the early days of promoting SuperJam, I would take my old 1973 VW campervan, Valerie, to these sort of events. I called her my 'Jam Mobile'. She didn't go very fast and would usually break down on the motorway on the way to a food fair, but when we finally got there people would love coming over to check out the little fête that we'd set up all around her. It was a nice way of creating a fun space in which to promote our brand and helped us to stand out at these hugely busy events.

TICKETED EVENTS

Perhaps you don't just want to attend events, but want to run them yourself. There's no reason why you shouldn't be able to get started with a concept for an events business in a couple of days. By creating an idea for your first event and a site to promote it, you could start attracting a crowd right away.

Eventbrite is a brilliant service for selling tickets to your events online. It allows you to create special discount codes and guest lists, and makes it really easy for you to keep all of your attendees in the loop about the event.

Running events always seems easier than it is – there are so many 'moving parts' that the potential for something to go wrong is very high. For your 48-hour start-up, I recommend creating something relatively intimate – aim to sell out a 50-person event rather than trying to stretch yourself to fill a 250-person venue. A successful, sold-out first event will make selling tickets to larger events in the future easier and will also give you a chance to test out your concept, learn what works and doesn't work, and iron out any 'teething problems'.

PARTY PLANNING

Maybe you don't want to sell tickets to your event but want them to be completely free. Rather than charging for entry, you make money by selling products to people while they are there. This is called 'party planning' and there are a number of enormous corporations, such as Tupperware and Pampered Chef, that have been built on the back of this form of direct selling.

The trick is coming up with a compelling enough event that people would want to come along to – for example, you could run a free wine tasting or host a talk by an expert on a particular topic. Once people have attended and enjoyed the event, they will hopefully be receptive to your business idea and, at the very least, will feel obliged to give your product a shot.

You could use Facebook to create an event and then invite all of your friends and contacts. And, just by using Facebook's inbuilt advertising system, you can easily pay for your event to be promoted to people that Facebook thinks would be interested in coming along.

CUSTOMER-REFERRAL SCHEMES

A lot of internet start-ups talk about their 'viral coefficient'. They encourage their existing customers to refer their friends and contacts, perhaps with incentives. If they can get to a point where each new customer who signs up refers more than one additional customer on average, their site will go viral and experience exponential growth. This is to say that their viral coefficient will be greater than 1.

Although this may sound an easy thing to achieve, it is in fact extremely difficult and it is unlikely your site will experience exponential growth. That said, it's hugely worthwhile figuring out ways that you can build customer-referral into the design of your site.

The most powerful recommendation is that of a friend, and if you can encourage your customers to tell their friends about your product, you will be able to acquire new customers very cheaply.

There are many customer-referral programs that integrate very smoothly with services such as Shopify. You can create an offer – for example, 10 per cent off for new customers. Existing customers who share this with their friends, who then sign up, will receive some kind of bonus for sending their mates your way.

AFFILIATE SCHEMES

Similar to a customer-referral scheme, an affiliate scheme allows your partners (for example, bloggers) to promote a link to your site, encouraging their own visitors to buy your product. If they click this special link, it will place a 'cookie' on their computer – when the customer goes on to place an order, the system knows who sent them your way. The affiliate company can then be paid for their help with a percentage of the sales that their link generates.

There are lots of affiliate management platforms on which to get your affiliate scheme started, and many of them plug in very easily to the likes of Shopify. Of course, the other side of the coin is that it is possible for you to earn money from the traffic visiting your site by placing affiliate ads for products and services that you think would be appealing to the type of people who are visiting. This is one of the main ways that free websites such as blogs and news sites make money.

DISCOUNT CODES

A very simple way that you can encourage people to place their first order with you is by generating promotional codes. If you are using a service like Shopify, this is extremely easy to do in the admin section of your account with them. For instance, you might create a code that gives people free delivery on their first order, or 10 per cent off if they spend over £50.

All you then have to do is let people know about the code – you could send it to your Twitter followers, put it at the bottom of your email signature, or perhaps partner with a blogger to allow them to offer a special deal to their readers.

If you have an affiliate scheme in place, you will also be able to submit your discount code to money-saving forums and discount-code aggregators. Examples include MyVoucherCodes, VoucherCodes, MoneySavingExpert and HotDeals. How these sites work is that they provide their subscribers and visitors with codes to get discounts on virtually any website on the internet, and when they click to reveal these codes they place a cookie on their browser. If one of their visitors places an order, you will owe them a slice of the pie, just as with any other affiliate transaction.

HOME TV SHOPPING CHANNELS

Throughout my adventures with jam, I've been to some fascinating places, but one that I never imagined I would find myself in was the studios of the leading home TV shopping company in the world, QVC. Television shopping is an often-overlooked medium for companies to sell their products and is certainly not relevant for every business, but it's worth knowing that many billions of pounds a year are spent by people sitting in front of their TV sets, buying products in this way.

Some people imagine that TV shopping channels sell low-quality products and give customers a 'hard sell'. The reality is that if they were to do this, they'd have a lot of angry customers returning products to them – definitely not something they want. So, in my experience, TV shopping channels have an extremely tight quality-control process.

What this means is that it will be impossible for you to go from idea to TV screen within 48 hours, but I do believe you can create a website and a prototype of your product to send to a buyer at a channel for feedback. You'll have some work to do to pass all of their quality controls but you could well find yourself on air within a month or two if they're excited by your concept.

Selling SuperJam through TV home shopping in both the UK and South Korea has been immensely successful for us – we have delivered our products to hundreds of thousands of customers' homes in this way. What's more, many times that number of people have simply watched our shows and learned about our products without necessarily placing orders there and then. When you consider the brand-building power of TV, you can definitely see how this form of selling can help to grow your business and get your story out there.

The reason this particular sales channel has been so successful for SuperJam is, I believe, that it gave us a great opportunity to tell a story. On a single show we have anywhere from eight to forty minutes to communicate our message – an eternity compared to the half-second of attention that a consumer might give to our packaging as part of their weekly grocery shop in a supermarket.

At the time I first sold my products on home TV shopping, I was the youngest ever guest on QVC. The show was at 11pm at night in November 2010, around the time that SuperJam was really starting to take off.

The process began with an audition – an opportunity for the show's producers to figure out if I would be comfortable telling my story on live television, and for them to give me some tips as to how to best get our message across in the time that would be available. After this, I was given a date for my first show. I was terrified – I'd never done anything like it at that point. But, as it turned out, there was no need to be afraid. The presenters are so talented and professional that they do most of the hard work – all I needed to do was tell my story.

In the many shows that have followed, I've certainly learned the power of TV home shopping and would strongly suggest that you don't overlook this opportunity for your brand.

PARTNERSHIPS WITH OTHER BRANDS

As you've learned by now, I love finding shortcuts or ways of growing sales by 'piggy-backing' on other people's efforts. In all of the businesses I have been involved in, we've grown sales by partnering with like-minded companies. With SuperJam we have worked with tea, biscuit and clotted cream companies to sell and promote our products. With Beer52 we have worked with wine companies, food-delivery companies and even pizza restaurants to promote our brand to people who are likely to like craft beer.

What I love about working with other companies to help each other out is that it doesn't cost anything. For example, we'll maybe place a voucher for a wine company in our beer consignments and they'll do the same for us. We both get a chance to promote our products to people who like buying alcohol, picking up customers for very little cost.

Of course, as you're just starting out, you don't have a customer base towards which you can promote a partner's products, so you may need to come up with a slightly different offer. Perhaps you can pay them commission for each customer they send your way, or even just send them some of your product for free. If what they're doing is complementary to your business, they might even be happy just to recommend it to their customers for free.

MEET-UPS

If what you are selling is relevant to a particular niche or community, a great approach to finding potential customers might be to get in touch with the groups and societies that meet up to talk about that topic. Perhaps you'll be able to partner with these events to promote your business, or go along to introduce your idea personally to people.

My favourite way to do this is using Meetup.com. This is a site where anyone can create a group for their particular interest and invite other people to join them for a drink, a meal or any other kind of event. It's a perfect way to meet like-minded people, and in big cities you will find Meetups happening for even the most obscure topics.

Aside from using Meetups as a way potentially to sell your product or service, you might find them a useful place to go to meet like-minded entrepreneurs who are working within your field, or just local entrepreneurs in general. Starting up can be a lonely journey, but it doesn't have to be!

THE LAUNCH OF AWESOME OATS

⏱ Day 2, 9:00am

Having stayed up late creating the bare bones of my website, today's main tasks are to shoot the finished product, upload the images to my site and then go about trying to find my first customers.

For the most part, I'm able to leave Alex – my food stylist and designer – to his own devices when it comes to shooting the product. I email the final label designs to a print shop near Alex's house, where they can be printed on high-quality paper for him to attach to the cardboard tubes, which were shipped overnight from the packaging supplier.

We have a call to confirm timings and exactly which shots we need to get today. He'll spend the next two hours shooting the products, calling me along the way to ask if what he is doing is along the right lines of what I have in mind; then I'll need a few more hours to edit them. Normally, you'd spend a couple of days on this type of project, but Alex has agreed to work super-fast to get the job done on time.

🕐 Day 2, 9:32am

While Alex is working on the photographs, I start work on producing my first batch of products and finding customers to buy them. Now that I have a finished label, cardboard tubes and recipes, I can turn my concept into reality.

Of course, once I start producing my oat mixes on a big scale, I'll find bulk suppliers for all of the ingredients. And, if things go well, I will even find a third-party manufacturer to produce the mixes for me on a big scale. But, in order to have a finished product on the shelves today, the quickest option is to buy the basic ingredients at my local supermarket and make up a batch myself at home.

🕐 Day 2, 12:55pm

Awesome Oats first stockist

Now that I have a finished product in my hand, about 24 hours after having visited his store with little more than an idea in my head, I head back to my shopkeeper friend from yesterday, armed with a case of product.

He laughs when he sees me and I explain that I've accomplished my mission. I let him know that I took on board all of his advice from yesterday about creating visually interesting but reliable packaging. When I show him the finished product he asks if it was really designed in the last 24 hours – 'It looks incredible,' he says.

Given his positive response to what I've created, I offer to leave the case of product with him for a week for him to try to sell. This first case is on the house whatever happens, but if the product sells well I'd love him to consider selling it on an ongoing basis.

 Day 2, 1:16pm

By the time I've had some fun making up my product and gluing labels onto cardboard tubes, Alex starts to send me the first shots that he has completed. I truly couldn't have wished for the product to look any better – the recipes look delicious and I don't think anyone would believe that the packaging designs had been turned around in a day.

The tote bags that I ordered with the Awesome Oats logo on them also arrive, along with some promotional stickers to go on the packaging of our ecommerce orders. This kind of extra merchandise will really help to make the delivery experience feel as professional as possible, and having these extra items helps when sending samples to buyers or the press.

I can start adding photos to the website. Later today Alex will send me his final shots, which I'll use to complete the site, but in the meantime I have everything I need to start setting up a Facebook advertising campaign.

Awesome Oats Facebook campaign

Day 2, 2:10pm

Advertising oat mixes on Facebook might not seem the most obvious place to go looking for customers, but since I want to sell my products online as well as in stores it is probably the quickest mechanism that I can use to start getting traffic to my site.

The cost of acquiring these first few customers is likely to be fairly high and I don't imagine that I'll make much money from them, but that's not really the point. I want to get some initial, 'real' customers to trial my product so that I can start getting critical feedback on the recipes, the packaging, the ordering process and everything else.

Assuming these first few customers like what I've created, they'll also hopefully start to post positive reviews, which I can incorporate onto the homepage of the website and also into the marketing for the brand.

With all of this in mind, I want to show you the basics of setting up a campaign. It really is pretty simple and Facebook's online tools walk you through it step by step. Of course, the total potential audience that you could advertise your product to on the world's biggest social network runs into the billions, but the point when setting up your campaign is to start by serving your ad to the people who are most likely to buy.

I begin by setting up a Facebook page for Awesome Oats, adding a little description of the business and uploading the couple of photos that Alex has sent me so far. The page looks a little sad without any 'likes', so I invite a few of my friends to like my new creation.

I don't really know who my target customer is, but I can take a good guess. I select that I only want my advert to be shown in the UK, to people between the ages of 25 and 35. I also select that I only want it to be displayed to people who have 'liked' the pages of my competitors; by entering a few of their brand names, I end up creating a potential audience for my advert of 82,321. By Facebook standards this is a pretty small group, but for the purposes of making my first few sales I can hopefully convince a few of them to order from me!

⏱ Day 2, 3:21pm

The ad isn't going to win any creative awards, but it hopefully is tempting enough to encourage a few 'clicks'. The ad gets sent for review by Facebook and after being approved it'll start being served to my potential customers. I'll just have to pay a fee each time someone clicks on it, which Facebook will deduct from a pre-paid account balance. The exact amount will depend on how well the ad performs, how sought after the people I am targeting are and a variety of other factors that are handled by their algorithm. How exciting!

While I'm waiting for that to happen, I finish adding the photographs to my website, ready for the first few customers to start browsing my products.

⏱ Day 2, 4:50pm

Pitching Awesome Oats to a supermarket buyer

Even though I want to use small, local stores and direct sales over the internet to test out my idea and get feedback on my product, ultimately it is of course my dream to see Awesome Oats on the shelves of major supermarkets. What I learned from growing SuperJam was that ultimately, if you want to build a sustainable business in the world of groceries, you've got to go to where your customers are – and that's in the aisles of the supermarket giants.

Given the premium price of my oat mixes, I figure it's best that I start at the top – with the UK's most high-end supermarket, Waitrose. Of course, I've had some experience of supplying them for over a decade, so you might be thinking, 'Hey, that's cheating – they're already your friend!'

While it is true that I have a great relationship with the jam buyer at Waitrose, the person who buys breakfast cereals probably has never heard of me. And besides, even if they do know all about SuperJam, they'll still treat my new project with just as much scrutiny as they would with any new supplier that contacts them out of the blue.

A lot of people ask, 'How can I get in touch with a retail buyer?' It may surprise you how simple the process is. I start by typing 'Waitrose breakfast cereals buyer' into LinkedIn. The buyer's profile appears and, given I now know her name, all I need to do is send her an email (firstname.lastname@company-name.co.uk), with some information about my project.

I provide her with a brief introduction to the story of how I came up with Awesome Oats; I was inspired by the success of super-premium oatmeal mixes in the US and figured there was an opportunity to bring something exciting to the otherwise fairly boring UK porridge category.

I let her know that I'd be delighted to offer this exciting new brand to her company on an exclusive basis for the first six months and ask whether she'd be up for meeting me in the coming week or two. I add that I'll be happy to bring some samples. Of course, if she does agree to meet with me, I'll have a bit of time to figure out how I'm actually going to produce these mixes on a big scale.

And there you have it: less than two days after I came up with the idea, it's in front of a buyer at one of the country's biggest supermarkets.

Whether she says 'yes' is another matter. Having seen this process before, I'd say the chances are that she won't accept my product straight off the bat. Perhaps I've contacted her at the wrong time of year for her to make changes to her range or maybe she wants to see some hard data about the trends that I mention I've seen in the US.

With any luck, though, I'll get a meeting and she'll be happy to give me some suggestions on what I need to do to get my product onto her shelves.

Awesome Oats first sale!

⏱ Day 2, 7:11pm

It's been a long couple of days and I wasn't sure at the outset if I would actually end up making a sale to a 'real customer'. Pretty much in the nick of time, thanks to my Facebook ads, someone has placed an order for one of each of my tubes. My first £11 is in the bank, so to speak.

I package up the order, ready to send it out from the post office tomorrow morning. I'm eager to find out what the recipient thinks of the package and the products inside, so I'll be sending them an email, maybe a week after they receive it, to ask what they thought and whether they have any ideas on how I can improve it.

Gaining my first customer cost some £80 ($118) in advertising, so I certainly haven't made a profit yet, but that's not really the point. Clearly, there are lots of channels that I can use to sell my products – whether small stores, supermarkets or more unusual mediums such daily deal sites and TV home shopping channels.

While the jury is still out on whether or not I can make Awesome Oats into a profitable company one day, what I have proven over these two days is that it is possible for anyone to create a product and take it to market in 48 hours.

I hope that the lessons I have learned on this journey and the steps I have taken will help you to shortcut, hack and otherwise expedite the process of turning your dreams into reality.

UGLY DRINKS

How to find your first customer

Entrepreneurs Hugh Thomas and Joe Benn turned their experience working at VitaCoco into an opportunity to create a brand of their own. They looked at the drinks fridges in stores and realised that most of what was on the shelves was loaded with sugar. On a trip to Tokyo, they discovered a range of

unsweetened bottled teas in their stores, and this got them working on creating a no-added-sugar range of sparkling waters to
launch in the UK.

These guys are great salesmen – as well as being super-
passionate about their product, they're great at not missing an
opportunity to make a sale. They recommend always carrying
your product with you – 'You never know when you're going
to meet Oprah Winfrey!'

When it comes to convincing a store to start stocking your
brand, they have some great advice on sales: 'The first step in any
sales process is to put yourself in the other person's shoes and try
to understand what they're looking for.' Having worked for an
American company, they learned early on how to get over their
British awkwardness about selling. 'Basically, it's about being nice
and understanding people.'

Joe worked hard to build relationships with potential stockists
over time, keeping them up to date throughout the process of
developing the products. 'A lot of people think sales is like pitching to a brick wall – but it's not, it's a two-way conversation.'

They recommend that the first step is to figure out what is
the route to market in your particular industry – whether your
new stockist will want to buy through a distributor or directly
from you. By taking a step back and asking, 'Why would this
store stock my product?', you can hopefully give them an answer
– but most of all, you can show your passion!

You can listen to the full interview on the *48-Hour Start-Up*
podcast show at 48hourstartup.org.

CHAPTER 8

WHAT NEXT?

It's been an exhausting time and I've amazed myself by what it has been possible to achieve in just a couple of days. I hope that you've enjoyed the ride and that it's encouraged you to set two days aside yourself to give your own 48-hour start-up project a shot.

Starting from just a blank page, I've been able to bring Awesome Oats into the world; a new brand with an online outlet and a retail customer that I think has the potential to one day become something more than just a homemade kitchen-table business.

If I do decide that I want to make a 'proper business' out of my idea, there's a number of things that I'll need to get in place. Although I wanted this book to be all about the first 48 hours of starting a business, I figured I'd be doing you a disservice if I simply waved you goodbye at this junction.

The journey you will go on from day three onwards is fraught with challenges and difficulty. Going from product to profitable business is not an easy road, but there are a few things I have learned along the way that I think will help you.

Just like for Awesome Oats, when you take your business on its next steps there are some things that you absolutely have to do and some that are up to you. As well as setting up a legal company with an address and a bank account, you may need to think about possible funding sources for future growth as well as for hiring a team to join you on your adventure.

I don't want to fill this book with the boring nitty-gritty of business administration; there are plenty of books you can buy on that! But in this chapter I'll give you a few pointers on how to spend the minimum amount of time on this 'boring stuff', so that you can spend more time on the fun stuff.

With Awesome Oats, if I decide to move production beyond the kitchen table, I'll need to find a manufacturing partner to produce my recipes on a big scale. Once the number of orders from my online store gets significant enough, it won't be possible for me to pack each order by hand and take it to the post office on foot any more. I'll need to find a 'pick and pack' fulfilment company to send my orders out for me. And, who knows, one day I may even decide to try exporting my products or setting up a charitable project to give something back to the community.

REGISTERING A COMPANY

It is possible that you can start trading without the formality of setting up a limited (incorporated) company and instead leave that task for later. You may decide just to run your business as a sole trader for a while, to see if it takes off – in which case, you just have to let the tax authorities know and pay tax on whatever money you make, as part of your usual tax return.

However, if your business turns out to be a success, it will be most tax efficient and safest from a liability standpoint if you register as a limited company. You can actually do this in a matter of minutes by using online company-formation agents, and it shouldn't cost more than £20 or £30.

OPENING A BANK ACCOUNT

In theory, at least just to get things started, you can run your business out of your personal bank account – just so long as you keep good records of all of the money that is coming in and out of your business.

It is best if you can open a business bank account as soon as possible and have all of your company's finances running through it. Unfortunately, many banks are pretty useless and this step will likely take a number of days to complete. Shop around, as some banks will offer you a free account for 12 months to get you to sign up, which will save you a bit of money in the early days of your business.

SET UP A MAILING ADDRESS

There is absolutely nothing wrong with running your business out of your home, and the chances are that is exactly what you will do. If you are concerned about your privacy, you may decide to set up a PO Box address.

These days, you're unlikely to get all that much mail, so you may decide to do away with having a physical address at all. You can choose to set up a 'virtual' address, which could be on a prestigious street like Pall Mall in London or Madison Avenue in New York.

How this works is that all of your mail will be sent to a mailbox on that address and then forwarded to your home address when you want it, creating the impression that your company isn't really being run from your bedroom.

Some services offer you the option of having your mail opened, scanned and emailed to you for a small fee. This is really cool because it means you can avoid missing any important letters even when you're out of the country.

GOVERNMENT GRANTS

One of the most frequent questions I get from people thinking of starting their own business is 'How can I get the government to help me?' I'll start by saying that if you think anyone other than you is going to start your business, you're really thinking about entrepreneurship in the wrong way.

If you come into this process thinking that it's someone else's job to fund your idea or help you find staff or anything else, then you're unlikely to succeed. It's entirely down to you to make your business a success – and any other help or financial support you manage to pick up along the way should be viewed as a bonus.

It's not the government's job to start your business for you and it's certainly not something you should suppose them to be any good at, so don't expect them to solve your problems for you.

It's very easy to spend an enormous amount of time trying to access government grants and other forms of support for starting your business. They usually come with the need to write an elaborate business plan and attend all kinds of meetings. In my experience, while very well intentioned, a lot of these schemes are going to teach you considerably less than just rolling up your sleeves and giving your idea a shot.

Having said that, you may well be eligible for funding for your idea and I'd be crazy to tell you anything other than to accept it with both hands. There are some online grant search engines that you can check out to find what funding sources might be relevant for you. It's also possible to find business plan templates and grant application templates online to save you creating the necessary documents completely from scratch.

If you decide to go down this route, you'll come across a lot of people who want to tell you how to run your business; people who've never actually started a business themselves but who are suddenly an expert. Just be aware of this fact and take everyone's kind advice with a pinch of salt. You should know that the best way to learn what you need to do is to spend time not with supposed 'experts', but with your potential customers, understanding how you can improve your product.

CROWDFUNDING

A lot of businesses, including our own, have used crowdfunding with great success, and this new type of finance really is an incredible opportunity for you as a start-up entrepreneur. It used to be the case that the only ways for you to raise money were from friends and family or from a bank or angel investor. But now, you can raise funds from anyone – your customers, your community and the public at large.

What's exciting about crowdfunding is that not only can you use it to raise much-needed finance to scale up your concept, but you can build an army of supporters around your cause.

One of the most successful crowdfunding stories comes from another set of Scottish entrepreneurs, BrewDog. You may well have come across their high-flavour, high-attitude 'punk' beers; their rise to success has been meteoric. It's a success that has in large part been down to their ability to build a 'cult' following around their brand, with the help of a number of stunts.

In their early days, if you got their logo tattooed onto your body they'd reward you with free drinks in their bars. They also produced the world's highest-alcohol beer; I think it was about 30 per cent alcohol. But then a little German brewery rose to the challenge and brewed an even stronger beer, stealing their title from them. So then BrewDog 'declared war on Germany', which is kinda controversial, right?

In the end they brewed a beer that was about 50 per cent alcohol, packaged it inside taxidermy squirrels, and sold it for around £500 a bottle. They were all over CNN and Sky News, and because of this and all kinds of other hare-brained publicity stunts (not to mention great products), they've built a huge base of fans around their brand.

One thing they did that I thought was really smart was to be one of the first companies to use crowdfunding in a big way.

Over the past few years they've raised many millions of pounds to build a new brewery in Scotland and even one in America.

But aside from being able to fund an incredibly aggressive expansion that has seen their sales grow to over £50m, they've turned tens of thousands of their fans into an army of 'super-fans'. Every bar they go into, they order BrewDog beer. And if the bar doesn't stock it, they ask why. They tell their friends about the brand and send in ideas for new bars and new beers to the company.

Partly inspired by BrewDog's experience, we have run several of our own crowdfunding campaigns, raising around £1m in total. Much-needed funds that have helped us to grow significantly faster than we could have done otherwise. Above all, we now have this community of people around our brand who bring more to the table than just money – between them, our shareholders have a lot of experience and contacts that we have been able to tap into.

If you're sold on using this new funding model to jumpstart your company's growth, there are a few things we have learned that will hopefully help you to run a successful campaign. First, it's all about the video; you need to be able to create a compelling clip that helps to get potential investors excited about your project. It needs to convey your enthusiasm – anyone watching it needs to be able to trust that you are the person to make this idea happen.

Your video is there to get people enthused about your idea – enough so that they want to download your business plan and financial projections to learn more about your project. In those documents, you want to include testimonials from experts as well as examples of your own experience and success to date. People want to know that the market you are operating in is big enough for you actually to build a substantial business within it.

These documents and your video can be uploaded quite easily to one of the popular crowdfunding platforms. Many countries now have their own equivalents, but in the UK the most popular are Crowdcube, Seedrs and Angels Den. These platforms charge a small fee, usually around 5 per cent, of the total that you raise. And as well as hosting your video, they'll promote your pitch to their fairly extensive networks.

In doing this, they'll hopefully be able to attract enthusiastic strangers to invest in your business. But as well as attracting strangers from 'the crowd', the success of your pitch will rely on your ability to bring your own network to the party – your friends, family, customers and social network all need to be aware of your funding drive. One great way of doing this is to download all of the email addresses of your LinkedIn contacts and send them a link to your crowdfunding page, with your business plan attached.

Assuming your fundraising is a success, after your campaign ends you should make an effort to keep your new shareholders up to date with developments in the company. Not only will they hopefully be able to give you some useful input, but they will also be much more likely to invest in a future funding round if you've kept them excited about your project along the way.

LICKALIX ICE LOLLIES

How to run a successful crowdfunding campaign

Dominic and Karis set up their all-natural ice lolly company, Lickalix, after making ice lollies for their kids and friends for a few years. They saw the success of 'ice pops' in the US and figured that maybe there was an opportunity to create a similar business in the UK. Then, after getting their homemade products into a few stores, they decided to use crowdfunding to help scale up their production.

In many ways, they saw it as the natural progression for their business – they knew that at some point they'd need to raise a lot of money to set up their own production and didn't want to give away too much control of the business. They didn't want to go on *Dragons' Den*, get kicked around on TV for entertainment and end up giving away 30 or 40 per cent of their company. A bank, though, really wouldn't touch such a small business; it's just not what they do.

They figured that crowdfunding would be perfect for a food business like theirs – it's a product that anyone can understand. They had also read about great incentives for investors such as the Enterprise Investment Scheme in the UK, where investors get 30–50 per cent of their investment back as a tax credit, helping to limit their potential risk. It seemed that convincing investors to come on board wouldn't be too much of a challenge.

In the end their crowdfunding campaign was indeed a huge success and they found themselves with more than 200 different investors on board. Since the campaign has ended, they keep their crowd up to date with an email every three or four months. They take the opportunity to invite their investors to suggest, maybe, a café in their area that they think could sell the products. One of the bigger investors also sits on their board, which has helped to bring some experience to the team.

Overall, crowdfunding has been nothing but a positive experience for Lickalix. Their tips for anyone wanting to do the same are pretty straightforward: 'A good video is really important – if I recommend anything, don't use one of those animations where you don't personally appear. It's really important that people actually see you and that your passion shines through.'

You can listen to the full interview on the *48-Hour Start-Up* podcast show at 48hourstartup.org.

FINDING TEAM-MATES

As well as potentially needing to find investors or other funding sources for your business idea, there's a good chance that you will need to hire some employees to help you as your business grows. It can be a huge challenge to attract the right people and to keep them motivated, but if you can do it well then it is ultimately this human force that will make your business succeed.

In a world where 'USP is dead' and your product most likely isn't that much different to those of your competitors, one of the things you can do is create a unique culture. By forming a team that is more passionate, more hard working and more entrepreneurial than the other companies in your sector, you can increase your chances of winning the race.

What I have found in all of our businesses is that by working on ideas that excite us and by creating products that we honestly would buy ourselves, attracting other people to join us is a whole lot easier than it otherwise might have been. People love working in businesses that have a soul, and typically do a great job when they're selling a product that they believe in.

When it comes to hiring people to join our businesses, we have never been fans of looking for the most-qualified, best-experienced person out there. Sure, it's important that the person we are hiring has some experience in the field in which we want them to work. But what always counts more to us than anything is that they're passionate about our brand and believe in what we're trying to do. If they're enthusiastic and smart, they'll be able to pick up the necessary knowledge and skills along the way.

In the early days, you may not have a huge amount of money to build a team, but you still need an extra pair of hands. Working with you on growing your business could well be a valuable experience for an intern, giving them a chance to learn about your industry by getting involved in your business. There are many sites, such as Enternships and Inspiring Interns, where you can easily post an ad for your company and invite enthusiastic young interns to apply to join you.

If what you're looking for is someone with a bit more experience, I personally favour a more direct approach. The chances are that your ideal candidate is already employed, doing the same role that you are looking to fill but at another company. If you draw up a list of the companies in your area where such a candidate might be working, it becomes very easy to search for the right people on LinkedIn. Just enter the job title and filter by your city and the companies you think could be a good fit.

There's a pretty good chance that your message will be warmly received – a lot of people are tired of their jobs and open to trying something new. And, what's more, if you're offering them a way to escape corporate life to join the exciting world of start-ups, you could have plenty of excellent applicants to choose from. Your only challenge will be offering a competitive salary, especially if you're trying to convince them to leave a well-paid job in a big company.

One way that you might choose to overcome this is by offering equity or share options in your company. I'm a huge fan of making sure that your team benefit from the success of the company – it helps them to stay aligned with the overall mission and also creates a much more loyal team. Finding people to join you in the first place is extremely hard, so giving them equity is one of the best ways of preventing them from leaving you.

EXPORTING

A lot of people will set out with grand ambitions for selling their products all over the world. It's only natural that as entrepreneurs we have these kind of dreams. Incredibly, barriers to selling your product across borders have all but disappeared. If you're running a purely online business, there's no reason why some of your first orders shouldn't come from outside of your own country.

If you are selling a physical product, however, my advice would be to focus on markets closer to home. For most businesses, the place that your business is most likely to succeed in is your own country, so that's where you should put your attention in the early days. If you can't make your product work at home, it's even less likely to succeed when you try selling in another country – with the added complexities of different currencies, languages and regulations.

Despite the challenges of selling overseas, it can be enormously rewarding doing so. With SuperJam, seeing our products on the shelves of stores in countries as far away from home as Japan and Australia has been one of the truly proudest aspects of building our business. Not only have I had the pleasure of getting to visit some pretty far-flung places; it has also brought large volumes of sales into the company.

The country that we have had the most success in has been South Korea, where we have been selling since 2014, with the help of a local partner. Before we started exporting our products there, I didn't really know a huge amount about the country – safe to say, I didn't have any explicit plans to sell our products there.

My last book, *SuperBusiness*, was translated into a few languages, Korean being one of them. A couple of Korean entrepreneurs, David Min and Hanbyeol Won, read my book and thought, 'Eureka!' They figured that SuperJam could really work in their market and got in touch to ask if they could sell our products there. 'Sure,' I said, since I'm always happy to give new ideas a shot.

They ordered 200 jars, then 2,000, then 20,000, and now we have sold many hundreds of thousands of jars of SuperJam in the country. Similarly, another entrepreneur – Jeanette Sorensen, in Denmark – heard about SuperJam back when we first started and, out of a huge love of the brand, has helped us to gain distribution there, acting as our brand manager.

What I've learned from the experience is that selling in another country is just like starting a business all over again – you need to start small. Just get your products into one or two stores, then grow from there. Don't make elaborate plans and procrastinate; just go there, get your product there and find your first customers.

There are all kinds of people who will want to help you on the road to exporting your products – government agencies, consultants and numerous other 'experts'. It can be a total minefield of well-intentioned people trying to help you join up the dots. But, just as with starting a business in the first place, I am a fan of taking action rather than talking about it. The world is unbelievably small. For £600 ($1,000) you can go just about anywhere in the world and get your feet on the ground. Call it your holiday. Stay with a local family for £30 ($50) a night with Airbnb and learn everything you need to know about your target consumers – ask them what they think of your business and how they feel you should get started in their country. You'll be amazed at how easy it is to make connections by visiting Meetups and other events for entrepreneurs – the global entrepreneurial family is a small one and everywhere I've been I've had no trouble finding people who can help me get my brand established there.

In my experience, whether you physically go to the country or just try making contact online, the most important person for you to find is a local partner. They might be an entrepreneur like my partners in South Korea, or they might be a company. You need to find someone who believes in your brand as much as you do – someone who you can trust with your baby. And when you do hand it over to them, it's important that you give them the freedom to customise your packaging, website and marketing to appeal to their own market.

Every country is different and you'll discover particular cultural quirks about each along the way, which is part of the fun. Some countries are easier to enter than others. Quite recently, we started selling our products in Japan, and I really wanted to organise a meeting with the major TV home shopping channel there. Despite trying my best to get in touch, I just couldn't get through to the relevant buyer.

In the end, I figured there was only one thing for it. I went to their office on my next visit to Tokyo, uninvited. I told the receptionist my name and that I had a meeting with the food buyer. A few moments later she asked me to confirm my name. 'No, I'm sorry,' she said, 'it doesn't look like you have a meeting.' After explaining that I'd flown all the way from London and that there really must have been some kind of mix-up, the receptionist conceded and called the food buyer.

A few minutes later, I had my opportunity. Thanks to a morning spent practising in front of the mirror, I very politely introduced myself and my company in Japanese, before exchanging business cards with a slightly confused-looking food buyer. Then I pitched my products to her before showing her a Japanese TV dramatisation about my life story on YouTube.

When I told her about the success we have had on other TV home shopping channels around the world, she apologised for the mix-up with the meeting and promised that they'd look into launching our products on their channel. She thanked me for making the trip and within days we were negotiating pricing and supply details.

I guess what I'm trying to say is that selling your products in another country is not that much different to selling them in your own country. You just need to go there, find people you can trust and in all likelihood put yourself out of your comfort zone a bit further than you usually would.

SOCIAL MISSION

For me, one of the really exciting things about starting your own business is that it can be whatever you want it to be. For some people, starting a business is about getting rich – and that's fine. But for me, what's way more exciting is that you can not only use your business to make a living out of something you love, but also use it as a way to bring about changes in the world that you feel strongly about.

Ever since I was in my early teens, I was inspired by the stories of entrepreneurs such as Anita Roddick, of The Body Shop. She proved that it is perfectly possible to build a hugely successful business without compromising on your personal values. She was also able to show that business can be a form of protest – you can use your packaging and advertising to shout about issues you feel strongly about and use your profits to fund causes close to your heart.

The most amazing feeling of my whole journey was the day I was able to go into a Waitrose supermarket and see SuperJam sitting there on the shelves for the first time. It was a moment I had been working towards for years, and it had finally come true. I still enjoy going into supermarket stores, especially in foreign countries, and seeing something that I created being put into people's shopping baskets. I love the feeling that millions of people have enjoyed my product – to me, that is success.

But what also feels like success is that we have been able to invest some of the profits we have made into setting up a charity. And to give you a bit of background: when my grandmother originally made jam, she'd make jam and scones and visit all of the elderly people in her area, who were maybe living alone or in care homes. She'd drag my little brother, Connor, and me along with her at the weekends – he'd play his guitar and I'd tell some stories.

As kids we obviously had no idea why our gran was doing this, but as I grew up I realised that it was something she felt strongly about. And so, when SuperJam took off, I thought it would be nice to do something like that on a grand scale. We started running completely free tea parties for elderly people in care homes, hospitals and community centres – originally just in Scotland but now all over the UK.

Over the past couple of years we've had many hundreds of parties. The biggest ones have had as many as 500 grans and granddads at them – so thousands of people have come along and hopefully had a great time. And they've not just been going on in this country – we've had a few in Australia and South Korea, and even one or two in America – although in America we don't call them 'tea parties'; it turns out that it means something different over there …

More recently, the big idea for our tea parties has been to open them up more widely, by making it easy for anyone, anywhere, to volunteer to set one up in their own community. We have a website – superjamteaparties.com – where people can apply online. We send them, of course, some jam, but perhaps more importantly a little money that they can use to hire a venue, hire a band and put on a really great afternoon.

When I go along to a SuperJam Tea Party and see hundreds of older people having a nice afternoon, knowing that I was a part of making that happen, it gives me a great feeling. It's also wonderful for everyone who works with me to feel that they are part of something that has a lot more meaning than just making money, something that is hopefully doing some good.

With these experiences in mind, I wanted to share with you the thought of creating a social mission for your venture. Not just because it's a nice thing to do, but also because it makes good business sense. Your customers will love you for it; people want to buy from brands that stand for something, that make a difference and that help to create a better world.

What your social mission should be is entirely up to you – it needs to be something that you care about. It's all the better if it relates to your products or is something that your customers are likely to care about too.

There are many ways that you could set it up; perhaps by establishing an entire project, doing some *pro bono* work for a charity or even donating a percentage of your profits to a good cause. You may want to adopt a 'buy one, donate one' policy, where for every product you sell, you'll contribute money or product towards your chosen cause.

Having a social mission will give you something unique to shout about in your marketing and, if it's tied to what your business does, it can help to strengthen your message. By supporting an issue that is close to your heart, you will be helping to make your company become more human, more real and much more appealing for people to support.

For me, it is inspiring to imagine that what may well begin as a two-day experiment, with a bit of love, hard work and support from the right people can grow into something amazing. Something that changes your life – I know that my projects certainly have changed mine. Something that gives you a career and, perhaps most inspiring of all, a chance to give something back to your community.

CHAPTER 9

RESOURCES, LINKS, TOOLS, PLACES TO GO, THINGS TO READ

Throughout the 48-hour start-up project, I have taken advantage of all kinds of tools that have made it possible to create a business at high speed. There are also lots of tools that we use every day in our businesses to look for new ideas, to communicate with our customers and to collaborate as a team.

Here is a list of all of the resources I have mentioned in the book, along with some other tools that I think you will find useful in running your own start-up. Links to all of these sites, as well as a variety of other resources, are available at 48hourstartup. org.

I'd love you to visit the site as your next port of call; I have been conducting interviews with all kinds of successful and start-up entrepreneurs, asking them to share their tips and tricks, lessons learned and advice for anyone on their entrepreneurial journey. The *48-Hour Start-Up* podcast features expanded conversations with some of the entrepreneurs I have mentioned in this book, along with several others.

As well as continuing to record interviews with some of my favourite entrepreneurs, I'll be updating the blog with stories from you, the readers of *48-Hour Start-Up*. I want to let the community know about the projects you have started. So please, don't let this be the end of our conversation – I'd love to hear how you get on!

Start-up accelerators

Y Combinator, Wayra, Seedcamp, Tech Stars, Launchbox,
DreamIT Ventures, SeedRocket, AlphaLab, BootupLabs,
Shotput Ventures, Capital Factory, 500startups,
StartupBootcamp.

Idea inspiration

TheNextWeb, Betalist, TechCrunch, FastCompany, Wired,
Springwise, Trendspotting, PSFK, CoolHunting, Startups.co.uk.

Design inspiration

TheDieline, LovelyPackage, Behance, Dribbble, Designspiration.

Crowdfunding

AngelList (global), Kickstarter (global), Indiegogo (global),
Crowdcube (UK), Seedrs (UK), Angels Den (UK).

Domain name registration

BustAName – enter words related to your idea and this will
generate possible combinations of domains that are available to
register.
NameStation – create a competition for 'the crowd' to come
up with your name.
GoDaddy – the largest domain registration site.
Sedo – the largest domain name auction site.

Intellectual property info

Ipo.gov.uk, USPTO.gov – check government-registered IP
and register your trademarks and patents.

Fonts

Fontfabric.com, Losttype.com, MyFonts.com,
YouWorkForThem.com.

Freelancer marketplaces

Upwork, Elance, YunoJuno, Freelancer, PeoplePerHour.

Craft marketplaces

Etsy.com, NotOnTheHighStreet.

On-demand merchandise production

Zazzle, CafePress, Spreadshirt, Everpress, Merchify, Supreme
Creations.

Finding Chinese manufacturers

Alibaba.com – the largest listing site of third-party
manufacturers in the world.

Self-publishing

Blurb, Amazon CreateSpace.

Designing and building your own website

Shopify, SquareSpace, Strikingly: 'drag and drop' website-
building sites.
ThemeForest – pre-designed website templates.
Balsamiq Mockups – create a quick layout of what you want
your site to look like.

Payment processors

PayPal, Stripe, GoCardless.

Subscription payment apps

Chargify, Sassy, Spreedly.

Offline payments

Square, iZettle, Shopify.

Hiring interns

Enternships, Inspiring Interns.

Stock photography

Shutterstock, Alamy, iStockphoto, Dreamstime.

Ask for advice

Clarity.fm – pay a small fee to talk to an expert over the phone.

Organise your team

Asana, RememberTheMilk, BaseCamp, Trello, Calendly, Evernote, Join.me, Slack.

Manage social media

Hootsuite, Scoop.it, Content Marketer, Buffer, IFTTT, Buzzsumo, Narrow.

Analytics

Hubspot, Moz, Brand24, Optimizely, Flare, SumoMe, Google Trends, Google Analytics, RankTrack.

Marketing tools

SurveyMonkey, MailChimp, WuFoo, SendGrid.

Customer service tools

Doorbell, Zendesk, Intercom, Help.com, Desk.com, Get Satisfaction.

Productivity tools

RescueTime, Toggl, Pocket, Google Drive, DropBox.

Accounting, finance and legal tools

Exact (cloud accounting software), Xero, Mint, Expensify, Wave, Yodlee, BodeTree, Bench, TermsFeed (create your T&Cs in minutes).

99Designs

Create a logo design competition.

CoFoundersLab

Find a co-founder for your start-up.

RECOMMENDED READING

These are just a few of the books that have helped me on my journey as an entrepreneur, as well as the titles written by entrepreneurs I have mentioned throughout the book.

- *Free*, Chris Anderson
- *Ben & Jerry's Double Dip*, Ben Cohen and Jerry Greenfield
- *4-Hour Workweek*, Tim Ferriss
- *Delivering Happiness*, Tony Hsieh
- *The Laws of Simplicity*, John Maeda
- *Confessions of an Advertising Man*, David Ogilvy
- *Start with Why*, Simon Sinek
- *Lean Start-up*, Eric Ries
- *Business as Unusual*, Anita Roddick
- *Smartcuts*, Shane Snow
- *Business for Punks*, James Watt

ACKNOWLEDGEMENTS

The 48-hour start-up project has certainly not been a one-man show and I must thank all of the people who have played a role in its success: Alexandre Paganelli for his incredible high-speed food styling and Sam Dunn for her world-class illustration skills. My agent Adrian Sington for believing in the concept right from the start, and Carolyn Thorne and her team at HarperCollins for bringing this book into the world in the most amazing ways. Thank you also to all of the other entrepreneurs whose advice I have shared throughout the book.

ABOUT THE AUTHOR

'My story shows that what can start as a passion, on a tiny scale, with love and hard work, can grow into something that changes your life.'

Fraser Doherty started his incredible business career at the age of just 14. After being taught how to make jam in his grandmother's kitchen in Scotland, he came up with a way of making jam 100 per cent from fruit. At 16, he presented his brand, SuperJam, to Waitrose and went on to become the youngest ever supplier to a major supermarket.

SuperJam has since grown into a company that has sold many millions of jars through thousands of supermarkets around the world. As well as being a commercial success, the business has invested in successful charitable projects – running hundreds of free tea parties for the elderly in Europe, South Korea and Australia and setting up numerous community beehives in the UK and South Korea.

Fraser is also the co-founder of Beer52, the UK's largest online retailer of craft beer (with sales of over £3m after just two years) and founder of Envelope Coffee, a successful fresh coffee subscription business that he exited in 2015.

He has been commended by the Prime Minister at Downing Street, by HRH Prince Charles, and was recently awarded an MBE 'for services to business' by the Queen. He has shared his incredible story at more than 500 conferences in 27 countries around the world, as well as in his first book, the bestselling *SuperBusiness* – published in the UK, South Korea and Japan.

Fraser regularly lectures in Entrepreneurship at universities around the world, including the London Met, where he is their youngest ever Visiting Professor.